AN OLD V. ~~~~~ ~
TAKE ON 2022 AND
ALL THAT

HOW EACH OF US CAN CONTRIBUTE
TO WORLD PEACE

DIANE ORTON

Contents

Chapter 1: Introduction..1

Chapter 2: What Is Joy?...12

Chapter 3: Sight...15

Chapter 4: Colour 34

Chapter 5: Hearing/Sound/Audition 43

Chapter 6: Touch/Tactile Perception..............................64

Chapter 7: Tactile Inner Sensations................................76

Chapter 8: Taste 91

Chapter 9: Smell 107

Chapter 10: Non-Physical Sensing................................123

Chapter 11: Chronicle 135

Chapter 12: An Ending 159

CHAPTER 1

Introduction

We're living in the strangest of times. Many of my friends are focusing on the turmoil and the seemingly unacceptable things currently going on in the world and they are fearful of the future. I do not share their viewpoint. Although I will be referring in this book to some of the disturbing events, it is my intention to focus on the steps each of us can take to make things easier for ourselves and for others during these unusual times. I'll be suggesting a number of ways in which we can help create the future we'd like to see.

All my life I've heard people talk about their wishes for world peace. The finalists in the Miss Universe competition would usually give that as their main wish when making final speeches to the judging panel, and it always touched a chord with the audience. Everyone wished for 'world peace', but most felt completely helpless. How could one person in so many billions make a difference?

Well, scientists tell us that we experience the world through our five senses, and I've learned that how we choose to respond to those experiences does make a difference to ourselves and to others. Moreover, we have much more choice than most of us realise in regard to what we 'sense' and thus experience. I truly believe that every one of us can contribute to a peaceful world—one in which all creatures live in health and harmony, and the planet itself flourishes.

In this book I will be writing about the usual five categories—what we see, hear, touch/feel, taste and smell—along with some of the 'non-physical senses'. I'll suggest ways in which we can all make simple changes that have the potential to bring enormous benefits to ourselves and to the world. While it's no longer accepted as truth that a butterfly flapping its wings can cause a typhoon, there is plenty of evidence that the radiations or vibes we are emitting do affect others. And our experiences and our responses create those vibes.

Today, due to advances in technology, people are more connected to one another than at any other time in history. My personal view is that we are even closer and that, in essence, we are one. I believe each of us is a divine being (spirit) experiencing life in the physical dimension. But that is not the subject here.

What I present to you in this book is a sort of Marie Kondo method of organisation and choice, but instead of dealing with clothes and material possessions, I'll be asking you to look at your experiences. You will be examining, in turn, everything that you are perceiving through your senses.

You may be aware that Marie Kondo, the world-renowned Japanese organiser, has written a number of books on organising and decluttering. Her system, which she calls 'the life-changing magic of tidying up', has transformed many people's lives. I read the original book when it was first published in English some twenty years ago and I promptly put into practice her advice to tidy by category — clothes, books, papers, miscellaneous and sentimental items — keeping only those things that speak to the heart and discarding all items that no longer 'spark joy'. Marie Kondo asks that we visualise the destination, follow our intuition rather than analysing or thinking, and let go of past and future attachments. She also mentions the importance of emptying our bag every day! I consider all of this advice to be just as relevant as we go through the process of examining and choosing (as far as is possible) our personal experiences.

My view of what is happening

I love analogies. They are especially useful when we're endeavouring to express the inexpressible. Analogies can give us an idea or concept where words fail or when what we are referring to is beyond our understanding.

I regard what is currently happening in the world as something that is truly beyond our understanding, and I've found it useful to liken the process to the major renovation of a house. A renovation is the improvement of a broken, damaged or outdated structure. It can refer to making something new or bringing something back to life.

When a house is being renovated, some of the structures might need to be torn out, removed and replaced. Walls might have to come down. It would look a mess. Staying in it during the changes would be challenging, to say the least. An onlooker could well believe that the destruction and demolition indicated 'the end'. But the architect, builders, etc. would know that it can all come together. They'd be aware that there might be unexpected delays and problems, but would be confident that the end result would be worth any inconvenience, and that it would, in fact, bring about a much-needed transformation.

I, like many others, am of the opinion that the extraordinary changes currently taking place on Earth are going to result in the most wonderful transformation of both the planet and its people. I sense, deep down, and without any doubt, that what is happening will result in what we would call 'Heaven on Earth'.

Last year I allowed myself to be caught up in analysis and judgement of some of the 'questionable' things occurring in the world right now. I commented on friends' Facebook posts only to have those comments removed. I became physically unwell. It reminded me that it's best that I stand back and remain detached. I do not want to be too close to that site where the demolition work is taking place. It's not necessary for me to keep looking at the details of what is happening, and I certainly do not need to make comments on the undesirable aspects of it.

However, I originally intended writing a kind of chronicle on the changes triggered by the COVID pandemic, so I'm including a chapter on some of the extraordinary events that have happened and are happening world-wide and in Australia where I live.

Another analogy that seems appropriate to me, is to think of the current changes in terms of childbirth—a natural process that will happen anyway, and not one that needs to be feared. Something wonderful and miraculous is being created, and we have the option of making it less painful for ourselves and others. Learning to relax and let go of fear, and focusing on our present experiences, can assist us in doing that.

Each of us is absolutely unique. I regard every person (indeed every creature) as having an essential place in the overall scheme of things. You could say that each of us is a tiny piece of an enormous jigsaw puzzle. Tiny, but equally valuable. Each different, but as they need to be.

Obviously, we are at various stages of development or evolution when it comes to our behaviour. However, if we consider another analogy—a fruit tree—we might observe it as a seed, a seedling, a mature tree, in blossom, with fruit, losing leaves, etc. We would not judge and criticise the seedling for not producing fruit, and we would not despair at the state of things when the leaves fell from a deciduous tree. We're aware that it's all part of a natural and amazing cycle. I believe that despite our seeming deficiencies, we're all doing what we can given our situations and experiences.

However, most of us are choosing our experiences out of habit. We're not always (or even usually) making conscious decisions about the things we look at, or the things we smell, touch, etc. And it really is time to take more notice of what we are doing, because we have much more choice than we realise—and with a bit of practice we can even acquire new skills and new habits that better serve us.

Learning new skills

The natural way a baby or child learns is by example— observing and copying the behaviour of others. We learn to speak by hearing others speak. If we see the people around us reading, we will be motivated to read. Studies of children brought up by animals have shown that human babies can even develop physical attributes such as hairiness and walking on all fours when that has been their only example.

I've been a piano teacher much of my life. If I had my time again, I'd probably train in the Suzuki method, which initially is all about imitation of the teacher and parent. Instead of the student being presented with musical notation to read, they hear and see the music being played well, and are assisted in reproducing those sounds on the instrument they are learning.

But regardless of the method, learning new skills or habits takes time and practice and patience. To be able to play golf, tennis or any musical instrument, to read, write, use scissors or knit—just having the desire, the intention and the expectation is not enough in itself. Practice is essential, and a 'teacher' showing how to do it by example is preferable, along with some instruction and advice. These days, of course, the teaching might well come from a book or video. It is never too late to learn, if you have the desire.

Changing old habits

Most of us, maybe all, have grown up with many bad examples. Even if our parents or care-givers were loving and not judgemental, society itself may have led us into habits that do not serve us—think of all the clever advertisers creating material designed to part us from our money.

It takes longer to undo and change learned behaviour than it does to learn it in the first place. Tennis players with a new coach might spend a long time learning a new grip on the racquet or a new technique for serving. But whatever we're learning or re-learning, it's important to bear in mind that 'practice makes permanent', rather than 'practice makes perfect'. The way we practice and the care we take when practicing is of the upmost importance. And we need to be gentle and patient with ourselves.

Our bodies are made of stardust

Emeritus Prof. Anne Green, former head of the School of Physics at Sydney University, a recent Companion of the Order of Australia, has mapped the Milky Way. She says that 'we're made of carbon, nitrogen and oxygen. All those elements were made in the central nuclear factory of stars. We are, in fact, made of stardust.'

Examination of a human cell using radiography, nuclear MRI and cryoelectronic microscopy has shown that we are each made of a mix of eighty-four minerals, twenty-three elements (including gold) and eight litres of water, all distributed through thirty-eight trillion cells. Scientists have said that our bodies are built from terrestrial spare parts, with recycled butterflies, plants, rocks, logs, firewood, wolfskin and shark teeth, swan feet and eagle wings, fish scales and snake venom, flower petals and stardust, all broken down into the smallest parts and reconstructed meticulously and intelligently into the most complex beings on the planet.

A few years ago I previewed a copy of a book written by an American scientist, Rizwan Virk. The title and lengthy subtitle give an idea of the subject matter. It's *The Simulation Hypothesis: An MIT Scientist Shows Why AI, Quantum Physics and Eastern Mystics Agree We Are in a Video Game.* Rizwan, and many renowned physicists, question what we call reality, and consider that a computer-generated simulated world would explain some of the strangest findings of quantum physics. I found his book extremely interesting, despite the fact that some of the scientific details were beyond me.

Human beings are said to be three-dimensional beings living in a three-dimensional world. We can see that things have depth, breadth and distance, and it appears that they are made of solid mass that we can see, touch, measure and weigh. But scientists have long known that seemingly solid physical items are actually made up of atoms and molecules, which contain tiny bits of matter and enormous amounts of space between them. I've seen it suggested that all other dimensions are in the space between the particles. I definitely have the sense that everything that *is* (past and future included), is beside and around us, and exists in the present moment.

Fortunately, we do not need to understand the amazing complexity of our makeup. Most of us have no idea how the waves vibrating in the air can travel vast distances and be received and seen as real-life moving pictures on our screens. We experience it, and accept it, usually without wondering about the process and how it is possible. I believe our bodies are designed in such a way that if we focus our attention on what we are actually experiencing, we will know what we need to know, when we need to know it. It will 'come to us' one way or another.

Our ability to receive and transmit

Being vibrational beings, our physical body is like a radio or TV in that it can *tune in* to the waves/vibrations in our environment. It seems we actually choose (usually unconsciously) everything we receive and experience. But we each have the ability to consciously change our vibrational level and control what we emit as well as what we receive. We can be so much more creative and powerful than we've been led to believe.

Being sensible/coming to our senses

It's all as simple as 'being sensible'—an expression greatly used in the past by parents, teachers, anyone giving advice (often unasked for) when they wanted us to be conventional and follow our head rather than our heart. Someone might have yearned to be a poet, a composer of classical music, a painter or an actor, but they were told that the sensible thing to do was to work in a field that gave them a larger and regular income.

I like to use the word 'sensible' and the phrase 'come to your senses' to mean quite the opposite—the awareness, *without any mental analysis*, of our faculties of sight, smell, hearing, taste and touch, and the huge range of 'sixth sense' or extra sensory perceptions available to us all.

An optimistic view

Knowing that many people are fearful of all that is happening in the world, I want to share my optimistic view of what's taking place.

I'd like to offer a potential antidote to the widespread concern, and that's to begin taking stock of everything we perceive through our senses. Focusing on the present is of enormous benefit. I believe that we can choose more enjoyable and valuable experiences, and, whenever possible, let go of those that don't bring joy.

As a result of making these changes to our sensory input, each of us will be able to function, or vibrate, at a level that will help others—and help the whole world.

CHAPTER 2

What Is Joy?

In the next few chapters I'll be asking you to notice which of your experiences spark joy. But what is joy? Is it the same as pleasure? Is it related to the so-called 'feel-good hormones' that flow through the body when triggered by something we see, hear, touch, taste or smell? Happiness is said to be a 'chemical event'. Is this the same or similar to joy?

I've come to the conclusion that 'joy' touches the heart. It is more than a chemical experience. It is more than momentary happiness or pleasure. There's most definitely a joy that comes from contributing to the well-being of others—whether people, other creatures or the planet itself. Maybe, at heart, at a soul level, our desire to care, to share, even to put ourselves out to help one another, is our natural way of functioning.

Having said that, it's worthwhile looking briefly at the various hormones or neurotransmitters that produce the happy or euphoric feelings in our bodies after our brains have received information from our eyes, ears, mouth, etc. We can beneficially increase the levels of them through diet, exercise, meditation, or spending time with people we care about. (Supplements are available, but they can have serious side effects.)

Dopamine, sometimes called the 'reward or pleasure hormone', is actually a motivating energy. It excites and activates us when we are anticipating something pleasurable. Its release is triggered by sex, shopping, looking at social media, emails or YouTube (even notifications of these on our devices can trigger the release of dopamine), video games, smoking, gambling, a little win—as well as by finishing a task, self-care activities, a new hobby, eating, quality sleep, laughter, listening to music, and *gratitude*.

Dopamine creates an intense feeling of reward which can readily lead to addictions, as with many of the anticipated 'rewards' we are left wanting more. Experiences that constantly trigger the release of dopamine can prevent us from spending more time with loved ones or getting on with other more rewarding activities or work. After reading *Dopamine Detox* (Thibaut Meurisse) I did a forty-eight-hour 'complete dopamine detox'. The banned dopamine triggers included social media, internet, movies, phone, drug/alcohol consumption, sugar in any form, games and puzzles, exercising and music. I definitely felt more peaceful during and afterwards and have been in no hurry to return to any of them.

Serotonin, the mood stabiliser or happiness hormone, brings the sense that all is right with the world. Our levels of serotonin are increased by exercise (the runner's high), a healthy diet, meditation, sun exposure, a walk in nature, being outdoors, and *gratitude*.

Endorphins, the pain relievers, are the body's natural painkillers. There are some twenty types of endorphins, and they mimic the effect of morphine. I've never forgotten an incident on holiday with new shoes — wooden clog-style. I unexpectedly had to walk for miles, and the soles of my feet were badly blistered. It was agony, but I needed to keep going and get back with my two young sons to where we were staying. Suddenly, and to my amazement, the pain was replaced by euphoria! I couldn't believe it at the time.

Endorphins increase pleasure and reduce pain. They are released when we laugh, eat dark chocolate or a delicious meal, fall in love, or have sex. We can increase the levels by exercise, meditation, making music (singing, drumming, etc.) and by the effect of ultraviolet light from the sun on our skin (it stimulates the release of beta-endorphins in the skin).

Oxytocin, the love hormone, can be released through touch, music, and exercise. While its main function is to facilitate childbirth, it is produced when sexually excited, when we fall in love, cuddle or hug someone, or sing in a group! Doing 'laughter yoga' leads to higher levels of oxytocin and lower levels of cortisone (the primary stress hormone) giving a greater sense of well-being.

14

CHAPTER 3

Sight

Scientists have spent hundreds of years trying to understand how human sensory organs work. *Science* literally means *the state of knowing*, so it is constantly changing as new knowledge comes to light. There is, and always has been, much disagreement among scientists. I used to think experts were infallible but I now know that the phrase 'scientists say...' needs to be taken with a grain of salt—despite the fact that I'm using those words in this book. Much more is still to be discovered about how our bodies function, the causes and treatments of many illnesses, and about our five senses—to say nothing of the so-called 'sixth sense'. However, at present scientists consider that sight is the most important sense, followed by hearing, touch, taste and smell. I will present them in that order, although obviously our senses work together most of the time.

***

When we are awake, it's most likely we are using our senses of sight, hearing and smell. And the sense of touch can be included, as we use it to sense the temperature of the air, to tell us if we're feeling hot or cold, need to relieve ourselves, are upset, in pain, etc. It's rare that our brain makes decisions based on the information from a single sense. The five senses work together to give us a complete picture of our environment, and one sense will often trigger another one—we only have to see a photograph of delicious food to salivate.

Sight or vision is what we experience when we look around with open eyes, when there is sufficient light. We mainly rely on sight for information about our environment. However, unlike our ancestors who only saw what was literally around them in their immediate environment, much of what we see is from other sources. It might be from newspapers or other written or printed information. Most of the world now has TV or access to the internet, so we may well be observing online, through words or images, what is happening somewhere else. What we see might have been edited, and could even be completely fake. The expression 'seeing is believing' is no longer appropriate in our society. Pictures are photoshopped, and videos can be edited to show things that didn't actually happen.

The mechanics of sight

Light particles (photons) are reflected off the objects around us and enter our eyes through the pupils. They are then focused on the retina, where two kinds of receptor cells work together to send data to the brain (via the optic nerve, which is plugged directly into the brain). If the light is poor, our eyes automatically adjust by dilating the pupils to let in the maximum amount of light. It's preferable, though, that we have plenty of light when reading, working or playing, as good light means clearer and more comfortable vision, and prevents eye stress.

Our brain forms a visual image after receiving the data from the optic nerve. So what we 'see' is actually our brain's interpretation of the light entering our eyes.

This, no doubt, explains why a hypnotic suggestion is so powerful and can result in surprising behaviour. The beliefs 'implanted' in the mind by a stage hypnotist can override the visual sensations and provide great entertainment to an audience. It really seems amazing that someone can look at an onion, believe it is an apple, and eat the whole thing with obvious enjoyment. I've seen that happen at a show.

What is beauty?

There is much truth in the saying 'beauty is in the eye of the beholder'. One person might regard a painting or work of art as beautiful, while another sees it as rubbish. Neuroscientists at a New York university have discovered that a work of art activates the same part of the human brain for each individual. However, our *appreciation* of beauty relies on the *experiences* already stored in our mind. The brain has areas of creativity, beauty, love, pleasure, value and judgement. It is an area of the brain just behind the eyes that lights up when we look something we find beautiful.

Various levels of seeing

Have you ever seen something but it's not really registered? Sometimes, we might realise there's a difference in a room or a person, but we don't really know what that difference is. Much of the time we do not pay much attention to what we're seeing. If shown a photo of a group of people, we may just see that it is a photo of a group of people. If we were going to be tested on what we could recall, we might see that the people looked alike and are probably family. We could guess at parents and adult children, for example. We would notice the outdoor setting, the background, the foreground, the particular colours of the clothing, trees, blossom, sky, clouds. A photographer would be aware of even more, as he has a different eye for it, along with specific knowledge.

If we can be aware (consciously) of everything our eyes are seeing—we can add a whole new dimension to our experiences.

When I began using a Gratitude Journal each morning, I found myself looking at my surroundings through 'new eyes'. I noticed the tiny bubbles moving across the floor of the shower, and found it fascinating and enjoyable.

One particular winter's morning, I turned on the heater and was sitting up in bed in my 'penthouse' apartment ready to do some writing for this book. Then, to my surprise, I wrote the following.

'I've just felt the air from the bedroom air-con unit on my forehead. I can see two red geraniums in the garden at the opposite side of the courtyard when I lift my eyes from the page. I see the strong movement of the leaves of the trees—there must be quite a wind today. I'm hearing a kind of humming noise in the background. Not smelling anything recognisable—but having thought of smell, my breathing has changed. It's become deeper.

The shapes of the tree branches are pleasurable to look at and ponder on. The pattern of the man-made tiles on the building opposite to mine is emphasised as the sun shines on it. I observe some glass panels here and there. There are fallen dead branches and leaves on the roof—the men will be coming to clear it again before too long. I see the beautiful circular 'orb' light near the geraniums. The shape contrasts so perfectly with the natural shapes of the shrubs and trees and the straight lines of the walls and roofs of the buildings. I'm noticing with pleasure the grey-green colour of the painted balcony fascias and railings.

The colour of the sky—seen in patches at the back, up high—is magical. It moves my heart, literally. I can feel the sensation in my body as I look at the blue. There are so many trees and buildings to my right and opposite that those glimpses of sky are small in comparison, making them even more significant. They are like highlights in a room—touches of something so special that they lift the whole scene, and fill the heart with joy.

A small bird just flew across the 'picture' I'm looking at. The same (or another?) just flew back the other way. I feel blessed and thankful for the experience, the morning, the day to come, with its endless options for me to choose from, in regards to what I look at, what I eat/taste, what I smell, what I listen to, what touch and movement sensations I will experience—a hand, wrist and arm massage? And what sounds shall I make? Shall I sing or laugh just for fun? I will certainly enjoy playing the piano as I do every day, despite arthritic fingers.

Today is such a gift.
Such an opportunity.
I'm bursting with gratitude and love'.

I decided to include this because we tend to take our surroundings for granted, and not see the beauty in what is in front of our eyes. A friend of mine recently was without internet service, and stated that they were cut off from the whole world. It was as if they'd lost everything of value.

The observer effect

In May this year I had some unusual and unexpected visual experiences after writing about the perception of beauty. During my morning walk, I was struck by the appearance of the flowers in the gardens of the houses I passed. Each flower looked absolutely stunning. Never before had I seen colours such as those I was now seeing in every single flower. Even those blossoms that were past their best seemed beautiful to me. My heart was almost bursting with joy.

It hit me then, that our visual experiences can be very much influenced by the way we are—it was like a Eureka moment. I had no idea that the intensity of colour and the beauty of an object had anything to do with the person observing it. *I'm now realising that everything we see, hear, smell or otherwise sense is in some way the result of how we are.* Could it be that the observer not only influences the object observed—they create it?

I've long believed that our differing points of view were the result of our different past experiences and 'inheritance'. But maybe we really can see and experience our world quite differently, if we choose to.

The 'new' science of quantum mechanics says that *the observer of an event actually has a measurable influence on it.* This 'observer effect' is due to the wave-like nature of matter, which means that particles can exist in multiple states simultaneously. When being observed, electrons behave like *particles* (instead of waves). When not being observed, they can behave as *waves*, passing through many openings in a barrier, and meeting again on the other side.

Does perception create?

The philosophical question of whether a sound exists if there is no one to hear it came to my mind following my walk with the flowers. 'If a tree falls in the forest and no one is around to hear it…'

I decided to look up the quote, and was surprised to read that a 'Treatise Concerning the Principles of Human Knowledge' (published in 1710) states *'The objects of sense exist only when they are perceived'.* That is extraordinary! Our experience of the whole world is through our senses.

What we see changes us

We are all different, and we will each interpret and respond to what we see in different ways—but the fact is that what we look at *can change how we are.* It can change the vibrations that we are automatically and unconsciously transmitting to the outside world.

Looking at certain things can produce 'feel-good' and beneficial hormones in our bodies—the blissful face of a contented baby, a happy playful puppy, the stunningly coloured bark of a 'rainbow tree' (Eucalyptus Deglupta), a clear night sky full of twinkling stars. Reading a book or watching something on the screen can be uplifting and thoroughly enjoyable. There are certain visually-sensed experiences that not only being bring inner joy—they bring out the best in us in our interactions with others. We might feel good for the characters. We might laugh. We've all heard the saying that 'laughter is the best medicine'.

There are other things we look at (including books and programs) that leave us feeling disturbed, ready to snap at others, upset—a clear sign that looking at them is not beneficial. For most of us, seeing people deliberately hurting one another is most distressing.

I recall many years ago reading a book by a Jesuit priest, in which he suggested we check how we are feeling *immediately after reading a book*. I do not remember the words he used, but he recommended evaluating the experience straight away and noting how we feel. If we do not feel uplifted, it's an indication that we need to avoid reading such a book.

Looking at our phone and devices

Many people look at their phones (or similar devices) for hours every day. Our eyes are being focused on the small screen as we communicate with friends and family and engage with others on social media or just look at what people have posted. We place orders for items we want to buy—from toothbrushes to concert tickets. We search for information on anything we want to know. We check the weather and the latest news, and most of us look at 'social media'.

Social media is often used to vent anger. I'm always surprised at the number of vitriolic comments. Despite the

Facebook 'police', there seem to be hundreds of untrue posts, and reading these comments can be quite disturbing. There are also a number of Facebook videos that are clearly designed to be frustrating. Very engaging at first, they take maybe thirty minutes to reveal what was apparently about to be revealed at the start. These certainly do not bring out the best in those looking at them.

I recently came across the word Doomscrolling. It's the compulsive urge to keep surfing the web/social media apps for *bad news,* and it's a vicious cycle that sucks one in further. New research from Texas University shows it is not healthy, and that it can lead to mental health problems, even physical issues. How much better it would be for us and others if we use our devices for pure entertainment or uplifting or informative purposes. It would also benefit our eyes if we closed them when we had the chance.

I never watch commercials during the TV programs I view. I usually press the mute button and do something else. But it's easy, if sitting comfortably, to just pick up the phone and check Facebook posts or emails or messages until the program resumes. I recently started to use that time to close and relax my eyes and quieten my mind—a mini-meditation.

When we begin to take notice of what we look at, it can be quite a wake-up call. I was actually surprised at the strength of my desire to look at Facebook posts from or about people I do not know personally. There's definitely a kind of addictive or hypnotic quality to looking at insignificant things on our screens. All those inane 'tests' of observation, the lists of things you've never done. I'm now aware that dopamine is the culprit. We get shots of this 'feel-good hormone' when we scroll. But the continued stimulation is addictive and harmful to our bodies.

Gaming

I enjoy (and hopefully benefit) from playing the Scrabble-type word games Sudoku, Wordle and Quordle on a regular basis. But I'm aware that many people spend hours each day *gaming*—a word new to people of my generation. Last year, when buying an office chair, I came across an online advert for an incredibly expensive 'gaming chair'. The reviews said it was perfect for hours-long MMO gaming while sitting in your underwear!

Changing habits

Having been writing about being more selective in what we see—especially in what we look at on the screen, I've been surprised to discover I need to work on it. Usually, when I make my mind up, my determination and strength of will brings it about. But I'm finding that on Facebook I've been scrolling through my feed, reading and responding to posts and comments by my friends, but unable to stop myself from also looking at posts about the Royal Family, celebrities or even totally unknown people. So I intend to consciously practise a new way of using my devices. (This was written prior to the death of her Majesty, Queen Elizabeth. I was most grateful that I was able to go online at that time.)

Some people say it takes twenty-one days to change a habit, but I believe anything is possible. It's not 'one size fits all'. Intention and time may be all it takes. But I'm glad I came across the Thibaut Meurisse book (mentioned in the previous chapter). After completing the forty-eight-hour 'dopamine detox', I made the decision to limit my time on the phone to essentials (e.g. shopping, paying bills), communications with friends, and reading my weekday email updates on world news (the Squiz). Having had just two days without constant dopamine stimulation, I've lost the desire to use my devices unnecessarily, and have been enjoying a more peaceful state (and a clear conscience).

Fun and games with vision

As a child I used to love the party game of 'Remembrance', where a number of small items were placed on a tray. The tray was shown to the guests for a certain length of time before being removed or covered. Everyone would then write down all the items they could recall.

In many card games, Observing and remembering which cards have been played is an important aspect of the game. SNAP calls for deliberately looking at each card as it is turned over. Such games, even today's Wordle, Quordle,

Scrabble, etc. involve the analytical brain and our eyes—
and no doubt, it's good for the brain, was well as fun.

Optical illusions

Colour, light and patterns can be used in ways that are
deceptive or misleading to our brains. Optical illusions
have entertained and confused people for centuries—and
they're currently popular on social media. A still image
will appear to be moving, or an image might be interpreted
in two different ways.

With these, our visual perceptions appear to differ from
'reality', but because most of us respond the same way,
these experiences are considered normal.

Hallucinations

What's not considered normal are hallucinations—
'experiences involving the apparent perception of
something not present'. They are considered the result of
mental disorder or the effect of a drug, despite the fact that
for some two thousand years many people have seemingly
accepted stories of visitations by angels, the sighting of
Jesus after his death, and the countless similar events
recorded in the Bible.

Seeing the impossible

I have had experiences where I have not only seen, but had conversations and lengthy interactions with people who seemed real, but who did 'impossible' things.

The most recent was about three years ago. That morning I'd had going through my mind the hymn 'Be still and know that I am God' (Psalm 46:10). I'd played it when a church organist. The words were in still my mind when I got into a train to travel to the next station for shopping. I noticed a woman carrying a large fabric shopping bag. It seemed that those words were written on her bag—I couldn't see it all, the way it was positioned. As I stood up to leave the train I saw that she, too, was getting out at my stop, and I noticed that she walked very slowly and awkwardly. I stepped out of the carriage ahead of her, went quickly down the steps, crossed two roads, looked back and saw that she was well behind me. Another block, and I walked into the supermarket—and there she was, at the fruit display with her back to the entrance. I passed by to get my bread, but kept watching with fascination as she selected items of fruit. By then, I'd seen the words on her bag quite clearly, and felt a strong desire to speak to her, though I was also reluctant to approach a complete stranger. When I was ready to leave, she was still putting fruit into her trolley, so I stopped, and we had quite a lengthy conversation. That woman was no different from any other person I've seen or spoken to. Yet, walking slowly and with obvious difficulty, she'd 'translocated' from way behind me to a place well ahead of me.

Our eyes can deceive us

I had an experience some seven years ago, at a time of great stress, when, after washing my car, I reversed it towards the back decking in order to use the vacuum cleaner for the inside. I didn't stop in time. I felt and heard the car connect with and mount the wooden slats. I managed to drive forward a fraction, then got out to examine the damage. One corner of the rear of my car was badly dented underneath. I felt it with my hand as a hundred emotions flooded my body. With a heavy heart I did the interior cleaning and returned the car to its usual position near the road. The next morning the car was in perfect condition!

Can objects or people become invisible?

I used to enjoy watching the TV series 'The Invisible Man' way back. Many years later I met a woman who lived in a college with many others. She told me that she could make herself invisible—she could choose not to be seen by the people who were around. If she was in her room in pyjamas and wanted something from the communal area downstairs, she'd just go down, unnoticed. I've wondered about doing that, at times, but I think my self-consciousness would have the opposite effect and make me more noticeable.

I've had the experience of 'not seeing' something that must have been there. I 'lost' a beautiful and favourite pen I'd been given. I'd placed it on the floor beside my notebook. Other people were present and they helped me look for it. We all left the room for a tea-break and, on returning, there was my pen, exactly where I'd put it. There's an expression 'can't see for looking', which is sometimes used when a person is flustered and frantically looking for something and their disturbance prevents them from seeing it. My brain might have been scrambled at the time, though I was outwardly calm. But all the *other people*? I've since spoken to friends who would also swear that an inanimate object had disappeared and reappeared—that when they looked, it was not there.

Communicating with what we look at

Thinking is not needed when enjoying visual beauty, though I enjoy thinking of the 'spirit' or essence of a tree as I look at it, and will sometimes find myself having a silent conversation. Whether or not there are nature spirits or devas in each natural object, an imagined conversation with what we are looking at can be uplifting.

* * *

What do you see firsthand that brings you joy?

Firstly, let's consider the things that you look at directly, *not* through print or on a screen. Think for a moment about how you usually start your day. What is the first thing you see or look at once you've opened your eyes? Perhaps it's a bedside clock, but then?

What do you see when you look through your windows? If you can see the sky, trees or other natural features, then make a point of really looking at them regularly. I find myself smiling just at the thought of suggesting you take one minute each morning to do this. I hope that doing it brings a smile to your face, too.

If you travel to work, you may have the option to look through the windows of public transport. Why not take the opportunity to really observe the sky, clouds, any birds, trees, flowers, etc.?

In free time, consider going to a beach, park, lookout or other natural environment to relax and look. Or you may enjoy live theatre, live concerts, watching opera, ballet, sports events, or performances at a local club.

If you have a garden, then you probably know the delight of seeing plants grow, bud and flower. A garden changes every day, and it can be a joy to work in, as well as to look at.

Inside your home, really look at what is around you — the decor, furniture and furnishings, light fittings, photographs, ornaments, etc. Check out each room and make a note of anything needing repair or attention. Whether you're consciously aware of it or not, its presence will impact and prevent peace of mind. So take action. Remove and repair the item or make arrangements for it to be done—or perhaps discard or recycle it. But keep it completely out of sight until it's been dealt with. Clean dirty windows and/or the wire screen. Maybe a 'spring clean' is called for. Consider what differences you'd make if you wanted your home to look its best for a prospective buyer or agent? Do this for yourself if you can. It is a joy to be in a clean, attractive environment.

What do you see indirectly that brings you joy?

This is where I suggest that you pay attention to *what* you are looking at in books, papers, magazines, photographs, and on the screens of phones, computers and similar devices—plus the movie screen. Begin by noticing your current choices in each category. Become aware of which activities are joyful ones—before, during and afterwards. You might like to make a written list and consciously make changes one at a time. Do whatever feels right for you to increase your number of joyful visual experiences. Be aware at all times of what you are seeing and how you are responding.

What about the *time* you spend on devices or screens? Would you prefer more time to spend on other things? That motivating dopamine release is so addictive! It might be well worth your while to spend less time looking at a screen, and more time enjoying friends, family and the natural world.

There's evidence that we benefit by not looking at devices, TV, etc. first thing each day. Perhaps a visit to the bathroom is necessary, but then it's the perfect time for quiet activities such as journalling, writing, meditation, yoga, walking or practicing an instrument. Devices, and finding out what's happening elsewhere in the world, can wait for a bit. If possible, make your well-being a priority at the very start of each day.

CHAPTER 4

Colour

Colour is an aspect of sight that is of such importance, I'm giving it a separate chapter. Colour plays a huge role in the way we perceive the world and in the way our bodies function. Just imagining a colour can affect us physically, as imagining eating a lemon can. And colours can evoke emotions and trigger reactions *subliminally* without us even being aware of it. The colours we look at (or visualise) can bring much joy into our lives.

Colour is electromagnetic radiation of a certain range of wavelengths visible to the human eye. What we see as colour is *the reaction of light with an object.* I find this a difficult concept—but an object itself is not coloured.

Hue, saturation (intensity) and brightness are the characteristics commonly used to distinguish one colour from another. Every colour has a different wavelength, as do musical pitches. In fact, some people see and attach colours to the different degrees of the musical scale—or different 'keys'. I've had friends with this ability, and as a child I associated colours with keys. In reading about this subject I found, not surprisingly, that people respond individually. Some associate yellow with the note E (as I have always done), but others see a different colour for E. However, each of us always has the same association of colours and pitches—that does not vary. Hearing colours is not an abnormal phenomenon, but it's not very common. Some people see colours when they look at *numbers* or *letters* of the alphabet, and others *taste sounds*, *see smells*, etc.

Colour perception varies greatly between species, but humans are described as trichromatic, as our eyes have three kinds of receptors (cones), which perceive green, blue and red. However, it's also true that our perception of colour is mediated by red/green, blue/yellow and black/white channels. Researchers say that we can distinguish between one million different colours (some suggest as many as seven million).

While our eyes can see in dim light, we can't distinguish colours unless the light is of a certain intensity. The colour we perceive most easily is green. The hardest colour for our eyes to see is blue.

I was surprised to learn that under identical circumstances the same object can appear red to one observer and orange to another, as our brains respond so differently to visual stimuli. Even those whose eyesight is exactly the same will have a different perception—each of us has a unique point of view.

A colour will be perceived differently according to what colour is next to it. And a change in size, shape or distance can alter the way we see the colour of two items of the same hue. If we stare at a colour for thirty seconds and then immediately look at a piece of white paper, we will see the complementary colour, the one that is its opposite on a colour wheel.

Colours chosen to influence us

Artists, advertisers and designers choose their colours wisely in order to influence us. Much money has been spent on researching and testing our responses to colours so that the packaging and contents of man-made products on shop shelves have the greatest eye appeal. We need to be aware that the most appealing-looking product might well be of poorer quality.

Colours in nature

In my opinion, the colours in nature are always in balance and full of beauty, and will give us pleasure if we pay attention to them. I find every sunset and sunrise brings joy, though some are more amazing than others. The colours of some birds, flowers and bark of trees is so stunningly beautiful that it will definitely trigger the release of 'feel-good' hormones. Last night I looked out my kitchen window, and the sky was completely purple — the colour of Jacaranda blossom. It was an extraordinary experience. I've never before seen that colour in the sky. It was exciting. I immediately went to the western side of my apartment and saw the same purple sky above a band of deep gold — the last indication of the setting sun.

The traditional seven colours

In ancient Tantric-Hindu traditions, the colour spectrum is represented in the seven main *chakras* or energy centres of the physical body—red, orange, yellow, green, blue, indigo and violet. It's always been believed that water droplets in the atmosphere break sunlight into those seven colours to form a *rainbow*. A *prism* similarly divides light into those seven colours.

However, in 2016, French meteorologists identified *twelve* different rainbow 'flavours' or colours, each with its own distinct characteristics. They found that the size of raindrops can vary, as can the angle at which we view a rainbow, influencing the colours we can observe. They also discovered that the sun's distance from the horizon was the greatest determinant of rainbow colours. If the sun is close to the horizon only red and orange will be visible; if it's high in the sky the colours will be largely blue and green. I'll be looking more closely next time I see a rainbow!

Colour associations

There are many common expressions with colour associations. *Green with envy* indicates jealousy. A *blue-eyed child* is a favourite child or one who has been blessed. A *scarlet lady* represents wickedness or sexual freedom. We are *tickled pink* when really pleased about something, and w*hite as a sheet* when shocked or full of fear. *Grey or silver-haired* is a symbol of age. But depending on one's culture, colour can have very different meanings. Some cultures get married in red, while some funeral processions are in white. National symbolism can be associated with colours, as can political parties and uniforms, etc.

In our culture it is generally accepted that the colour red is associated with love, energy, passion, war and anger, while blue and green represent peace and healing. White, the colour made up of all colours, signifies purity. Black, of course, is the absence of colour.

Black and white are balanced and combined beautifully in the yin/yang symbol—a circle divided into two halves by a curved line. One half of the circle is black (yin), the other is white (yang) and each has within it a small circle of the other colour. This ancient Chinese symbol is an illustration of how opposite or contradictory forces may be complementary, interconnected and independent in the natural world. According to this philosophy, the world is thought to be composed of opposites: dark and light, male and female, earth and heaven, death and birth, matter and spirit. The symbol represents balance and harmony (dark side and sunny side).

Do we dream in colour?

It used to be thought that most people's dreams were by nature in shades of grey, and that seeing colour in dreams was rare. However, nowadays, scientific studies of REM have 'proven' that we tend to dream in colours, but we do not always recall them. My eldest son when young, used to look forward to going to bed as his dreams were like technicolour movies; he saw a different and enjoyable one every night. When I think about my dreams, I'd say they're neither colour nor black and white. I'm there in the dream as a participant and it 'feels' very real, but there's no sense that I'm looking at it and seeing it.

Using colour to bring joy

Many of us are in a position to choose most (if not all) of the colours in our homes. The colour of the things I look at in my immediate environment is extremely important to me. A tiny splash of colour can make all the difference to the way I feel when I walk into a room. My spare room contains a black piano with two black piano seats, black desks, a large black printer and a black-framed computer screen. When I moved here, there were full-length grey curtains at the window. I didn't feel drawn to being in the room and didn't like the 'feeling' or look of it. I took down the curtains, which let in more light. But the thing that made the room 'inviting' for me — that brought joy and still brings joy every time I enter the room — is a $4 artificial flower arrangement in a tiny glass vase on the desk, close to the piano. The jar-shaped container holds three azalea-type flowers streaked with deep and light pink with touches of white. They are backed by nine greyish olive-green leaves. It's quite extraordinary that seeing this can bring such joy all the time.

But then, I feel joy when I select which coloured peg to use when I hang my washing to dry! I would not mind selecting the pegs randomly—it's not a compulsion—but I get extra pleasure from spontaneously matching or complementing the coloured plastic pegs to the colours of the items. Purple with purple, deep pink with light pink, maybe blue with white. There are so many simple ways we can be creative with colour. I've always liked to match the outside colour of my pen to the cover colour of the book I use for writing.

When gardening, I used to select plants with an eye to the overall colour of the bed.

***

What colours bring you joy?

It's interesting that we can travel to other places and photograph sunrises or sunsets, yet take them for granted when at home. Even if it means going outside, consider taking a little time on a regular basis to enjoy the natural beauty of these colourful phenomena. If you're lucky enough to live where stars can be seen in the night sky, then take the opportunity of enjoying their twinkling light from time to time. The moon, too, can be a joy to observe, especially when it's full or new—and it's all free.

Cut flowers and/or foliage bring nature's colour and beauty into our homes. They can change the look and 'energy' of a room for the better. Many hotels and restaurants have a small flower arrangement on the dining table, but at home, apart from the occasional 'romantic dinner', I suspect it's rare for fresh flowers to be on the table at mealtimes. If you have a garden, you might experiment with a small centrepiece or vase.

Take time to observe the colours around you inside your home. Consider ways you might make the rooms more attractive, more restful, more suitable for creative work. You might add some simple touches of colour—and change them from time to time. Check out the colours of your tea towels and oven mitts in the kitchen; towels, washers and bathmats in the bathroom; throws; bedding; cushions; curtains; artwork and ornaments. Enjoy choosing or changing the colours you look at every day.

Some women wear the same colour makeup, lipstick, eyeshadow, etc., all or much of their adult life. If that's you, you might enjoy a different 'look'. You could even have a free makeup/makeover at a cosmetic counter at one of the major department stores and let someone else make the suggestions.

Last, but not least, give consideration to the colour of your clothes. Do you have items where the colour is not flattering to you or you don't even like the colour? With online ordering, that can easily happen. Maybe pass such items on. Only wear the colours you enjoy and look good in. When you feel good about the way you look, you will benefit and you will radiate joy.

CHAPTER 5

Hearing/Sound/Audition

Sound, or audition, is what we experience when our ears respond to vibrations of a certain frequency. What we hear can bring great joy. It can contribute to healing and even save lives. Mystics have long believed that sound holds the key to the creation of the universe, and that it can create spiritual as well as material change in our lives.

Sounds can be constructive or destructive. They can alert us to potential hazards and keep us out of danger (car horns, smoke alarms, train whistles). But you've no doubt heard the story of the opera singer shattering glass when hitting a particular high note. It is, in fact, true. In 1988 it was proven that sound can make, break or re-arrange physical structure. Loud sounds trigger our 'fight-or-flight' response and are physically disruptive in many ways. They can be quite damaging to the body. I found it interesting seeing little Prince Louis putting his hands over his ears during the fly-past over Buckingham Palace during the celebrations of Queen Elizabeth's Platinum Jubilee. He was instinctively protecting his hearing and well-being.

Sound waves are *heard* when they come into the *ear*, message the brain and result in various physiological changes. But sound waves can also enter the body at a *cellular level*—the sound source may be directly in contact with some part of the body.

Helen Keller lost both her sight and hearing when she was a baby aged nineteen months, yet she was able to experience great joy from the sound of Beethoven's Ninth Symphony by placing her hand on the speaker as the recording was played—clear proof that we can sense sound waves without using our ears.

This kind of sound experience is known as vibro-acoustics and it is now an approved therapy for increasing circulation, relieving pain and helping with mobility. It is currently being evaluated for many other conditions, including fibromyalgia, cerebral palsy and Alzheimer's disease. Ultrasound treatments are used to heal wounds, mend fractures, unclog blocked arteries and even shrink tumours. Sound- and vibration-focused practices are being rediscovered by modern medicine, as researchers learn more about the benefits. Sound might well become the medicine of the future—whether heard through our ears or otherwise sensed, it can seemingly relax our bodies and allow natural healing to take place.

The mechanics of hearing

Sound waves are a form of mechanical energy. Each sound wave has a unique frequency, measured in cycles per second (Hertz of Hz). There are many sounds we can't hear or detect, as our range is only up to about 20,000 Hz (though babies can hear higher sounds, and dogs can hear up to 65,000 Hz). The vibrations are received by the ear (auricle) and funnelled to the ear drum (tympanic membrane), which is at the end of the ear canal. The waves are amplified by tiny bones attached to the side of the ear drum, then travel through tubes (cochlea) where the movement of fluid across the hair cells in the ear generates nerve impulses that are sent to the brain. It sounds complicated, but the conversion of sound waves to electrochemical nerve signals happens almost instantly. Our brain then interprets the signals as dialogue, music, laughter, etc. If we hear the voice of a loved one or the tune of a favourite song, the parasympathetic nervous system is activated, releasing feel-good hormones and sending messages of safety, relaxation and normal functioning.

Our hearing is the very last sense to go—the auditory nerve functions until the very end. So even if someone is unconscious or in a coma and unable to respond, they can still be comforted by the sound of a loving voice or their favourite music.

Different qualities of sounds

When we hear any sound from nature or a voice or musical instrument, we hear harmonics—geometric multiples. The different harmonics are what create the different quality, timbre or colour of a sound.

The loudness of a sound is measured in decibels (dB). Normal conversation is about 60 decibels, but using earphones 110 dB is possible. Sounds above 70 dB over a period of time can damage hearing. Immediate harm and permanent damage occurs above 120 dB. The more *gentle sounds have the most powerful effect* for good. It's recommended that we listen to music at as low a level as we can hear it.

The benefits and power of music

Having been involved with music all my life, I'm particularly interested in how musical sounds affect us. There's certainly some history indicating its important benefits. Chant therapies were part of *medical practice* in ancient Egypt when music was considered 'medicine for the soul'. Wind chimes have been used in Nepal and around the world for thousands of years; in Nepalese culture they are often used to promote positive energy and ward off evil/negative energy.

Before the second century BC, Indian scripts told of links between man, music and the cosmos. The ancient Greeks considered music beneficial for emotional disorders. Pythagorus played an ancient form of guitar and stated that specifically prescribed use of music could benefit one's health. He pioneered the mathematical and experimental study of music, and influenced Aristotle, Plato, and later, the Western world. During the Middle Ages, music was played in hospital wards in Cairo (using voices and stringed instruments).

Music and royalty have long been connected. In 1737 the Queen of Spain engaged the services of the famous Italian singer Farinelli to rouse King Philip V from his acute melancholia. It was so helpful that Farinelli was employed by the king to sing to him every night!

The official use of music or sound as therapy began in June 1950, and since 1977 music has been used to reduce anxiety in medical settings in hospitals for both patients and operating personnel. Of course, lullabies have been sung to babies to soothe them to sleep from time immemorial, but many people now consider music therapy to be 'the newest thing in medicine'. It's anticipated that people will be doing sound healing together—that, in the future, there will be sound healing centres in hospitals, communities and schools.

Music makes us feel good. There's scientific evidence that it triggers the release of a range of feel-good hormones and activates the social networks in our brain. The greatest benefits seem to come when we make music together. In a choir, for instance, if the singers breathe together, heartbeats are synchronised, and the collective response is powerful. I still remember the level of happiness and the feeling of well-being I experienced when singing with a group at sunrise and sunset each day at aboriginal spirituality camp some thirty-two years ago. Our individual voices combined to create the most beautiful sounds I've ever heard, yet each of us was just being spontaneous in choosing the pitch of the note as we sang. We took quick breaths when necessary so that the sounds seemed continuous. We comfortably and intuitively changed pitch when we felt like it.

Today's worldwide interest in the use of sound for healing has given rise to many books and courses on sound therapy. And there are instruments galore, though any of them can be effective. Drums, singing bowls and gongs are some of the more common ones. An unusual instrument I came across this year is the tuning fork. Dr John Beaulieu is an expert in the therapeutic use of them. He says that, within seconds, tuning fork techniques can bring the body into a deep state of relaxation and peace. They activate the release of nitric oxide. Beaulieu teaches techniques said to alter the body's biochemistry and bring the nervous system, muscle tone and organs into harmonic balance. The sounds from tuning forks can help neutralise viruses, bacteria and other free radicals. I certainly enjoyed the sounds produced in his free online demonstrations.

For my birthday this year I was given the book *Waking the Spirit* by Andrew Schulman. This beautiful and extraordinary book is a personal account of how hearing the sound of his favourite music brought the author from the brink of death. It was considered a medical miracle, and it led to the classical guitarist dedicating his life to playing to similar crucially ill hospital patients. From the beginning, he wanted to know about the science behind it, so this book contains a great deal of compelling scientific evidence to support the view that music can comfort and heal. One of the interesting facts that he learned was that cognitive scientists have proven that *thought* takes place not only in the brain, but also in the body and in the environment around us.

The value of music education

Extensive research has shown that music education can improve literacy and numeracy skills and boost students' attention, focus, self-regulation and overall academic achievement. Learning music also enhances their wellbeing, motivation, love of learning, sense of belonging and connection to their school community. Every aspect of the school experience is bolstered by the increased cognitive capacity.

Many studies have shown that children who learned music performed at least a year ahead of their peers in language acquisition and syntax, and experienced up to a three-year gain in auditory processing that supports reading development. Yet only about a quarter of our government schools offer continuous developmental music education.

I was delighted to read a recent document from the headmaster of Canberra Grammar School, Justin Garrick. He intends to make music central to the curricular and extracurricular life of all pupils, with a new auditorium, new concert hall, four acoustically designed classrooms, and eighteen instrumental or vocal tuition rooms.

'In my school, we are putting music education literally front and centre', he began. He pointed out that music education should be for all, because music itself is for all. It's an expression of culture and is pervasive to our daily experience. He said that music surrounds us on the airwaves of radio, television and streaming, and influences our thoughts, moods and choices. We exercise, drive, shop, eat and celebrate with music. It's intrinsic to our wellbeing, social interaction, our spiritual and sensual experience, and to our religious, national and cultural rites.'

Sounds we make with our voice

Voice is formed by a vibration of air moving through our vocal cords, and it's shaped by our physiology, emotional state, intention, history and habits. So each voice is unique. Many of the sounds we hear are created by our own voice, whether it's by speaking, singing, humming, chanting, crying, screaming or laughing.

I recently read that our voice reveals a holographic picture of our health. Evidently the individual frequencies within a voice can be captured, translated and sorted into a voice print chart, giving a highly accurate indication of physical function in our body. It's also said to be helpful for emotional issues. A computerised program for this diagnosis was developed by Kae Thompson-Liu, and is used by many naturopaths and physicians. Analysis can even be done online with Zoom or over the phone.

Be careful what you say

At times, the words that come out of our mouths express the very outcome we do not want—and that's the message the brain receives.

'You do that again, and I'll…' screams the desperate mother in the supermarket.

I've even heard, 'You cry again and I'll hit you so hard …'

Only yesterday, I did a similar thing myself. I was booking a ticket online for someone else on one of those sites where there's a time limit. I encountered numerous problems with both the website, passwords and my internet connection. Just as I thought I'd succeeded, I noticed that I'd booked two tickets instead of one. I kept saying 'Don't time out on me', and, of course, it did. The person who wanted the ticket ended up visiting the concert venue to purchase it. We need to bear in mind that our brain is like a computer, in that the information it receives determines its response—the constant messages it sends to every part of our physical body.

Using our voice to bring joy and harmony

Our bodies love the sound of our voice, even if we don't. The power of *self-created sounds* (singing, chanting, humming, mantras, toning, laughing) has been recognised for millennia by ancient wisdom holders of various traditions, and it has been validated by modern science. These sounds deliver major physical and psychological benefits, and are enjoyable to make and/or hear.

I've always been self-conscious about my singing voice. But I do believe that singing and humming are of great benefit to us physically, so I've been doing my best to sing from time to time. I've enjoyed singing with others in choirs for most of my life, but singing alone is a very different matter.

Since the COVID pandemic began, I've taken advantage of the numerous online singing workshops our local council has organised. I've been pleasantly surprised at the improvement in my sound each time, when I've done the physical and vocal warm-ups, then joined with others to sing in harmony. It never fails to bring joy to me—I'm not too sure about the resident of the apartment below.

Humming is a way we can create sound without embarrassment. No one complains about being a bad hummer! 'Conscious humming' which is done with the intention of being of benefit, has been shown to lower blood pressure, benefit the heart, and release hormones that make us feel good. It triggers the release of nitric oxide which allows more oxygen to flow through the blood vessels. And it is good for the sinuses—try humming with your nose pinched.

Jonathan Goldman, a leading pioneer in the field of sound healing, has written a book *The Humming Effect* on the power of this self-created sound. He says that while humming may be one of the most powerful natural abilities we possess, most of us are completely unaware of it. His book contains a number of exercises, along with information on proven physiological benefits from validated research.

Before beginning to hum it is best if we relax, focus on breathing through the nose and into the belly/diaphragm, and then make the sound as we exhale. Humming stimulates the vagus nerve—a kind of superhighway that comes down the neck close to the vocal cords, carrying messages from the brain to many parts of the body. Thus humming can be a useful tool to calm us if we're extremely upset.

Laughter is a self-created sound that truly is 'the best medicine'. Laughter prevents stress and can be most helpful before any performance. In the 1980s and 1990s, studies were done that showed the benefits of laughing. There are documented medical benefits, both physiological and psychological. *Inner laughter* is another option—though laughing out loud is best.

Laughter yoga

In 1989 I attended a residential 'laughter weekend'. My main memory of it is how much my face hurt from smiling and laughing all the time. In recent months I've done some of the free laughter yoga workshops presented online by Mirthy, and I've definitely felt the benefit. It's a strange session of 'laughing like nobody is watching — just for the pure joy of it and to boost your mood, health and resilience.' It combines laughter with breathing and stretching exercises, and is described as 'aerobic exercise for the heart', so not to be done by people with heart problems. I was surprised and delighted to see an Australian TV documentary on laughter yoga recently. The participants had measurements taken before and after participating, and in every case their stress levels were reduced — and it was obviously a lot of fun.

Sound healing

Laughter was a subject included in the online Sound Healing Summit this year. I've registered and attended (through the Shift Network) three of the four annual summits held so far. They are free and can be watched live or on replay.

The presenters of the laughter video were experienced and trained musicians and vibrational healers. Their recommendation was that as soon as we get out of bed in the morning, we spend fifteen minutes laughing while gently stretching the body. 'The rest of the day will be so much better', they said. I tried that once—and only once. I did enjoy it, but I'm at my best in the morning, and I was keen to get on with other activities. But I do recommend smiling whenever possible.

When humming or toning for sound healing, specific parts of the body can be targeted. To target the brain, you might put your hand/s on your head, hum, and feel the vibration. You could visualise a colour as you do so. (Start gently with short hums followed by rest periods.) To begin, take three slow deep breaths to stimulate the vagus nerve and relax. And at the end, it's essential to spend a *short time in silence and stillness* to experience the vibrations. People are rarely aware of the silence after the sound, but it is literally as important as the sound itself for healing. It is in the silence afterwards that the experience of the sound will come and be encoded in the body. Silence is considered mandatory for sound healing—it's so important.

Sounds inside our head

We all hear sounds that have not been detected by our ears, and they do not fit the category of 'clairaudient'— beyond the reach of ordinary experience. We hear sounds from inside our heads. And there seem to be many levels of this.

I very often have a song or other music going on in my head. I can suddenly become aware that a particular tune has been in my head. I can then consciously listen to it continuing/repeating. I can also choose to 'sing it' internally. I can also deliberately choose a song or piece of music to 'hear internally'. And, as a musician, I can see some written musical notes and hear them in my mind.

All these sounds are sensed differently from sounds generated outside us.

Last year I was concerned, when after playing the piano or listening to recorded music, the music had stopped but I kept hearing the last sounds of it, exactly as it had been — not just 'in my head'. The sound was exactly as if it were coming from outside. For some years I've had hearing loss, and I feared this might be a sign of further deterioration. I looked it up online. To my surprise, my 'problem' was an indication of a great sensitivity to sound, and was considered an attribute.

I've heard many people complain that they can't get a tune out of their head, but I've always found that the words of any songs that come into my head uninvited are always relevant, and worth noting. I'm perfectly comfortable with them.

Some people can hear a piece of music for the first time and remember it well enough to perform it or notate on paper. By just looking at a musical score, some musicians can hear all the sounds of that piece of music — even if it is for a full orchestra. Some of us seem to be born with 'perfect pitch' and can hear a sound and name the corresponding musical note name/s. Some learn to acquire perfect pitch. Others haven't a clue. 'No ear' for music. 'Tone deaf'. They were told at school to mouth the words but not sing.

It's interesting that such people, in the hands of certain singing teachers, can learn to sing most beautifully. They can experience 'being in the moment', the release of feel-good hormones, and the sense of profound physical and psychological well-being. I'm currently reading a most interesting book, *The Singing Cure* (Amanda Lohrey), where the writer sat in on lessons by such a teacher. Lohrey says 'we don't need to sing in the way that we need to eat or drink or procreate and yet for many of us *singing is one of the most satisfying experiences of our lives*'.

Cymatics

This is the study of the visualisation of sound. Most of us don't actually *see* sound, but sound can definitely influence and create form. Being a type of wave, it can be displayed through visual media as matter reacts to sound, forming shapes and patterns. I remember many years ago seeing the most beautiful patterns in sand made by various sounds. Water is another medium where sound waves can be seen. Japanese scientist Masaru Emoto wrote of his research and experiments in the book *The Hidden Messages in Water*. His findings are so radical that many mainstream scientists discard them. But Emoto's photographs of frozen ice crystals over a period of more than ten years seem to show conclusively that the molecules of *water are affected by our thoughts, our words and our feelings*. And we are mainly water—our brain 75%, our heart 79%, our liver 86%—and overall, 60% of our weight is water.

Sound and plants

I remember back in the 1960s reading about experiments on the effect of sound on plants, and learning that the frequencies of musical sounds can influence a plant's growth. Birdsong is supposed to be about defending territory and raising chicks, but I've read that the song of birds triggers tree growth. I believe that to be true, though I've not found recent evidence to prove it. It has, however, been shown that sound waves can improve plant immunity against pathogens and can increase their tolerance to drought.

Sounds that we choose to listen to

For most of my life I've loved having classical music playing in the background when at home. From teenage years, when radio transmissions were limited to 6 a.m. to 10 p.m., I had a radio beside my bed and enjoyed falling asleep listening to classical music, then being wakened by it when the radio came on the next morning. Later in life, when living alone, I would sometimes wake during the night and the radio beside my bed would provide interesting and enjoyable words and sounds. I have always played recorded Christmas carols while writing Christmas cards—it's something I enjoy and look forward to every year.

Nowadays I prefer silence unless I am specifically listening to something, though I've recently learned that living alone in absolute silence (apart from when I play the piano) is not beneficial to my hearing. So I'm now deliberately choosing to listen to some music each day, and I'm paying more attention to the sounds around me.

Irritating sounds

Just as some sounds relax and calm us, and others energise us, there are sounds that irritate us beyond words. These days, the sounds of electric drills, motorised lawn mowers, leaf blowers etc. often interrupt and disturb. The good news, however, is that if we give full attention to an annoying or undesirable sound or noise—not think about it, but listen intently—then that *sound changes*. We actually hear it as pleasant. Our perception is changed through focusing fully on the sound.

I was amazed when I read about this maybe forty years ago. It's worked for me and for those I've told about it—a friend who lived in the flight path in England, a son who'd moved to a home on a very busy main road and couldn't get to sleep because of the traffic noise, and my own encounters with a screaming and distressed baby on an aeroplane. It's quite extraordinary and wonderful how such a simple change in the way we listen can seemingly change that sound completely.

Sounds we make using instruments

Everyone can use simple musical instruments like drums, tambourines and other untuned percussion. Some of us have acquired the ability to play piano, strings, brass, woodwind, harp, etc., which require particular skills. For those of us who are able to play either for ourselves or for others, music making can be a most joyful and nourishing experience. Performing music with others adds an extra dimension, and the happy memories of it can last a lifetime. For many years now, accompanying others on the piano has brought me the greatest joy. Even now that I'm playing alone, my time at the piano brings me much pleasure.

***

What sounds bring you joy?

What steps can you take to make and listen to pleasing sound experiences?

If you are one of the many people who wish they had learned to play a musical instrument—or, if they'd learned for a while, wish they'd kept going—it's never too late to learn. And there are many local groups for 'easy to play' instruments, like ukulele or drums, where you can make music with others.

Why not begin regularly singing or humming in the shower, where the environment makes your voice sound better? It's a great boost to the immune system, as it oxygenates the blood, reduces stress levels and lowers blood pressure. You might start regular humming or chanting to get the feel-good hormones flowing and quieten your busy mind. There are a number of free or low-cost courses available online if you'd like to be guided.

If you like to sing, could you join a choir of some sort? Not far from where I live there's a choir where members sing only the tune and do not need any prior experience or musical training. It caters for people with dementia but is open to all. Another local choir is for those like me who can read music and like to sing in harmony.

What about having a *sound bath*, where you completely relax your mind and body as you soak up the sounds of certain instruments? This could be live at a venue or by immersing yourself in a recorded or online live video performance.

Are you aware of the sounds you hear at the start of your day? Many people wake to the sound of an alarm clock or a person or a pet needing their attention. Can you make a point of listening to your favourite music in the morning and/or end of the day?

Are you able to wake naturally? I discovered many years ago that we can 'program' ourselves to wake at a certain time. We do not have to be shocked out of a deep sleep by an alarm. There are many methods, but the one I use (when it's essential) is just before sleep, I tap my head on the pillow a certain number of times. Six taps for 6 a.m. Six-and-a-half taps for 6.30. It's just a way of informing the brain of what I want. When I've travelled by plane or a once-a-day train, I set a clock alarm as well. But I've always woken just before the alarm, and turned it off.

I suggest you take notice of every sound you are hearing today (at least). Notice how your breath changes with each sound you listen to. Do you respond differently to natural and man-made sounds?

Listen to the sound of your feet on the floor or ground, the sound of the water when you turn on a tap, even the sound of your breath. I recently wore hearing aids for a few weeks, and I was astonished at these everyday sounds. The birdsong, when I went outside, was absolutely beautiful.

Think about what sounds please or displease you. Begin to be more selective when making choices. Experiment with making some changes, but do make sure you spend time in complete silence whenever you can. The silence between sounds is perhaps more valuable than sound itself. If you're one of the many people who wear earphones much of the time, you might consider using them less often and paying more attention to the natural sounds around you.

And, finally, if *you* are creating sounds, do bear in mind that the experts say that feeling joyful while making a sound, makes a difference—that sound will be more beneficial to you and to anyone listening to you.

CHAPTER 6

Touch/Tactile Perception

Touch—tactile perception, the haptic sense—is experienced when a part of our body is in contact with someone or something. Even the tiniest physical contact can send messages to the brain and cause major changes in our body's function. The word *feel* refers to our becoming aware of a person or object through being touched—though it also is used in a broader sense to refer to inner body sensations and emotions. Those 'inner feelings' are the subject of the next chapter.

Touch is the first sense to develop in a foetus and some say it's the last of our senses to go. We can't live without it. We are designed to touch and be touched, and it is essential for our emotional, mental and physical well-being. While sexual touch is necessary for survival of the species, 'skin hunger' is said to be even stronger than the desire for sex. Our cells record and can relive moments of touch.

It is through our tactile sense that we are able to detect changes in our environment and within the body. Our body signals are of utmost importance for our well-being. Touch also helps us recognise objects, discriminate textures, and communicate with one another.

The mechanics of touch

Tactile sense receptors are located in our skin, joints, ligaments, muscles and fascia—the connective tissue that holds every organ, blood vessel, bone, nerve fibre and muscle in place. The fascia is almost as sensitive as the skin, and it tightens up when we are stressed. The nerves that detect touch send their information to the brain, where the perception of touch, temperature, body position, pain, etc., takes place.

There are specialised nerve cells for the different touch sensations. The skin on our fingertips, for example, has different touch receptors from the skin on our arms and legs.

The fingertips can detect changes in texture and pressure, such as the feeling of sandpaper or pushing a button. I find it quite extraordinary that pianists can have such an influence on the sound they make just by touching the piano keys in a certain way. Using a mechanical instrument, a good musician can give and receive much joy as a result of depressing and releasing the piano keys with their fingers (and maybe some depression of the pedals with their feet).

Our arms and legs are covered in skin that best detects the stretch and movement of joints, and it also sends the brain information about the position of the body.

Our lips and the bottoms of our feet have skin that is more sensitive to light touch. In reflexology, pressure is applied to specific points on the feet (also ears and hands) in order to bring relaxation and healing.

Our tongue and throat have touch receptors that tell the brain about the temperature of our food or drink.

Skin brushing

Skin is the primary sensory organ for our sense of touch. It is also an eliminating organ, acting as a supplemental filter to the kidneys for removing wastes from the blood. Daily dry skin brushing with a natural bristle brush or loofah has a massage effect, and helps with both stimulation and elimination. It relieves stress and gives a feeling of well-being. Body brushing is said to release toxins, remove dead cells, unclog the pores of oil, dirt and residue, exfoliate, brighten, and tighten the skin, and help it absorb nutrients. It also helps reduce cellulite, increases blood circulation to the skin, stimulates the lymphatic system, increases energy and restores the skin's natural beauty.

And it's enjoyable. I've found it takes less than two minutes to brush from top to toe without hurrying just before I get into the shower each morning. I bought a new brush recently, and it came with two extras—a pair of exfoliating gloves to use in the shower, and a little face brush. I absolutely love the feel of the gloves as I rub my hands over my body, and the face brush feels so nice on the skin. It definitely brings me joy when I use it, and I think my face is looking better.

The importance of physical contact with others

During the COVID pandemic, many of us have been deprived of physical contact. I've certainly missed hugging my family members since March 2020, but they are concerned about giving me the virus. Hugging can trigger the brain to release oxytocin, which makes us feel good and lowers anxiety and fear. Like many others who live alone, my main physical contact has come from my hairdresser and dentist. There's actually a condition called 'touch starvation', which is recognised as leading to depression, withdrawal and anxiety. I've not experienced depression or anxiety, but I've definitely been more withdrawn in recent years.

I learned a lot about touch from the book *The Power of Touch* by Phyllis K Davis. I only wish I'd known earlier just how important it is for babies and young children to receive lots of loving touch. I don't think I ever propped up a baby's bottle so they could drink without being held — but I was of the opinion that their *main* needs were sleep, food, exercise, fresh air, sunshine and such — with no awareness that being held, touched and stroked was perhaps of greater importance for their well-being.

Davis mentions that back in the thirteenth century there was an experiment in Germany to find out what language a child would speak if it was raised without hearing anyone speaking. The nurses caring for the babies were forbidden to talk or touch them, and every baby died before they could talk.

Only sixty years ago in the USA, the mortality rate was almost 100% for babies under twelve months who were raised in an orphanage where the 'experts' recommended 'no handling except for necessary cleaning and feeding' in order to prevent 'spoiling'.

Fortunately, research has now shown that it is not possible to spoil a baby by holding it in order to satisfy its needs for safety and love. Slings and carrying devices where babies can be in physical contact with the mother or father's body have been shown to contribute to their physical and emotional growth. There's actually a way of carrying a prematurely born baby called Kangaroo care, or K-care, where the baby is placed upright between the mother's breasts *inside* her clothing. It's standard practice in some countries, and has been shown to benefit the babies in many ways.

Recent studies on the best ways for a mother to soothe an unsettled baby showed that the most effective strategy was picking up the baby, walking around the room holding them for five minutes without stopping, then sitting down and holding them for another five to eight minutes before settling them down to sleep again. Being carried by mothers in 'transport response' has been found to help the young become more docile—and not only in humans. My grandmother was right after all! Unfortunately, I followed Dr Spock's advice with my first two babies, and they slept in a room far away from us.

Touch combined with rocking is said to stimulate the heart and help with circulation. The old rocking cradles were ideal. Pacifiers (dummies) provide pleasant tactile sensations for babies and are now considered beneficial, though when my first adopted child began sucking his thumb, the clinic suggested a wooden splint on his arm to prevent him doing it. Twelve years later, the midwife who was with me for the births of my natural children described thumb-sucking as 'nature's pacifier' and welcomed it.

Stimulating a baby's sense of touch also stimulates their brain. My youngest child had Down Syndrome and I followed the advice given to gently massage her limbs and body with oil, every day. I'd not been aware that in some countries this is normal practice for all babies and young children, as it benefits both child and mother—giving a massage stimulates the tactile areas of our brain. Tactile stimulation for babies can also come from rattles, stuffed animals, blankets, pillows and other 'feel pieces'. These days there are some lovely books for babies where each page has pictures to touch and feel—rough, hard, soft, velvety and satiny textures.

A touch experience I remember from childhood is the sensing of static electricity. It comes from high-voltage ions and occurs within or on the surface or between materials.

It can be seen as well as felt if one is in a dark place. As children, we regularly combed our hair in the very dark toilet room at the end of the verandah at a friend's house and enjoyed watching the sparks fly and feeling the electrical charge.

Touch and society

Touching is culturally learned behaviour, and these days in our society, there's much concern about inappropriate touching and sexual harassment. As a result, there are many limitations on touching. I remember that as a carer, when helping someone to dress I was 'legally' required to ask permission each time I needed to make physical contact.

In many preschools touching has become taboo. Yet in a study of children from fourteen months to five years of age, where the preschool staff gave a fifteen-minute 'rubdown' each day, the children clearly benefited, becoming more alert and sleeping more deeply.

We do still have some accepted ways of touching one another. It's fine to dance with another, shake hands, kiss on the cheek, pat on the back, or embrace in greetings and farewells. We can touch when fighting, disciplining or playing contact sports. It's OK to touch others if we're grooming them—applying sun lotion to someone's back, tying bows or ties. And obviously, everyone accepts the professional and necessary touching by a hairdresser, dentist, massage therapist, beautician or doctor. There is also the indirect, vicarious touching we experience when we watch other people touching on TV and in videos.

I'm reminded that when I was young, the first things a doctor would do with a patient was feel their forehead (which gave him information about our body temperature) and look at their tongue. How times have changed. Even before the pandemic, some doctors had no physical contact at all with their patients. They looked at the computer screen while asking a couple of questions, then wrote a prescription or a referral.

There have been many medical advances during my long life, but when I was young, it was normal practice for doctors to visit the home. If someone was unwell, they could stay in bed and rest or sleep until the doctor arrived. It was so much better for everyone, as I'm sure the doctors were better off 'doing their rounds' rather than sitting at a desk in front of a computer all day.

Exercise

Way back in the 1960s I was in the local library and noticed a book called *How to Live Forever* (or something similar). I assumed it was a facetious title — not to be taken literally. The author was a medical doctor and I was intrigued. I borrowed the book and read it thoroughly. My memory of the details is very hazy — but what struck me and has always stayed with me was the author's claim that, in order to function well, our bodies need certain kinds of movement on a daily basis. Some of our organs, glands, etc., depend on being squeezed or otherwise impacted by us bending, twisting and stretching. As I remember it, it wasn't about the type of exercising done these days in a gym or using exercise equipment. And it wasn't about reaching perspiration point. Yoga, with its 'spinal twist', was considered ideal, but games such as tennis and golf, activities like gardening and, dare I say it, housework were said to provide the kinds of body movement necessary for our physical bodies to function at their best.

When I was checking the details of our 'feel-good' hormones, I was surprised to learn that exercise can trigger so many of them—as does laughter.

Massage

We do not need scientific evidence to know that massage can relax us and make us feel good, but the pressure of massage actually decreases the production of the stress hormone, cortisol, and increases the production of feel-good hormones. Until COVID, I enjoyed regular massages and considered them an indulgence. I now realise that having a massage is a way of caring for our health, and not an 'extra'—especially for those of us who live alone.

Earlier this year I bought a firm foam 'neck and shoulder relaxer'. It was recommended for poor posture, especially for those of us whose heads are forward. I noticed in the reviews that it also worked well for neck pain and headaches and was enjoyable to use. I absolutely love it. I can feel the happy hormones flowing when the back of my neck presses on the foam. I look forward to my ten-minute daily session, flat on my back on my bed with my eyes closed and my head supported by this oddly shaped item.

* * *

What tactile sensations bring you joy?

There are many tactile experiences you probably don't even notice. The feel of the water on your skin when swimming or in the bath or shower. The different feeling of cold water or hot or warm. I've read that just splashing the face with cold water stimulates the vagus nerve, releases feel-good hormones and benefits the body in many ways. Do you enjoy the exhilaration of being out in the rain, and that lovely comforting feeling of coming from the cold into a warm and cosy room?

You can add to the joy in your life by becoming aware of the many small everyday sensations, as well as the more obvious ones. Become conscious of how your body responds when you apply oil, ointment or cream to your skin. Let it be an opportunity to enjoy the sensations as you stroke your skin and apply different degrees of pressure. Even the feel of the towel when drying yourself after a shower can be enjoyed if you pay attention. A soft face-brushing brings joy.

Consider having regular massage, reflexology or similar tactile experiences. Make sure you do some regular stretching, twisting and bending—whether in an exercise regime or everyday activity such as gardening.

Most importantly, if you live with others, think about discussing the whole subject of touch and each one's needs. I strongly recommend you read the Davis book I mentioned—but whether you do or don't, I urge you to consider the various ways you might engage in physical contact with others to bring more joy to yourself and to them. And do not forget your pets. Stroking them will benefit both you and them.

What about your clothing? Many garments are not comfortable to wear, and it's something to consider when selecting what brings you joy. These days elastic is used in the waistband of many items including pants of all kinds (undies, pyjamas, track pants) and in skirts and trousers, and they always seem too tight/small. Even on slim people they can feel constricting. It used to be that men and boys always wore braces to hold up their trousers. They didn't have to use a belt. And for young girls the skirts were attached to a simple bodice. Comfort has been sacrificed in many instances, so it's helpful to pay attention to the comfort factor when choosing clothes and other items that come into contact with your skin/body. Does what you are wearing right now feel comfortable against your skin? Are your clothes tight anywhere? Decide if you need to make any changes.

The texture of fabrics can also give pleasure. When you are buying clothes to be worn regularly, or bedding, throws and cushions, consider the *feel* of the item. For me the feel is at least as important as the appearance. The softness of a cashmere jumper gives me joy when I touch it—as do the less expensive fleecy or velvety jumpers, jackets, dressing gowns, etc. Make a mental note of the textures you enjoy, considering not only the finger-feel, but the feel of the fabric against your body. You could recycle and replace items that do not bring joy, or just keep it in mind when next making a purchase.

CHAPTER 7

Tactile Inner Sensations

This chapter looks at our emotions, messages from the body, and breath—three extremely important tactile experiences.

But first I want to briefly mention EMFs (electric and magnetic fields). These invisible waves exist in a spectrum of frequencies that include radio and TV waves, microwaves, X-rays and radioactive elements. Our phones and other wireless devices communicate using these fields. There are also natural sources of EMFs such as sunlight, infrared, ultraviolet and visible light.

Our brains, hearts and nervous systems are the most obviously electromagnetic parts of our bodies, but every cell has an electric charge. Some believe that a high degree of electromagnetic absorption can change the electric current in the body. Manufacturers advise that we do not have phones and similar devices too close to our bodies and that we use 'speaker' phone when possible. Some people recommend disconnecting from wi-fi when not actually using it, switching devices off overnight or having them in a different room and unplugging the TV if it's in the room you sleep in.

There's much disagreement on this subject, but some of us are ultra-sensitive and experience physical discomfort from man-made EMFs. I personally choose to limit their use and I use a product designed to neutralise their effects. It's something to consider.

1. EMOTIONS

An emotion is energy in motion. It's a movement within us that can be pleasurable to the point where it becomes uncomfortable or so distressing that we can't go on as we were. We may lose control and say things we later regret. We may cry and withdraw. My grandmother fainted at 'bad news'.

Experiencing emotions is an essential aspect of being human, and by far the best response to an emotion is for us to feel it—even welcome it if we can, whether it's good or bad. It's just energy expressed in different frequencies. Ideally, we feel an emotion without judgement and let it move through us as we focus on *feeling* it and *allowing it to be.* I know that many people believe there's a need to 'work on' emotions, but I feel very strongly that these feelings do not need to be analysed or 'mastered'. They just need to be acknowledged and felt.

I did have an interesting and valuable experience, though, when I had a conversation with my fear one morning. I don't recall the words, but I'd made these notes. *I was loving in my approach, and the fear was so touched. Had not expected that response from me. Had only been trying to help. When it left—dissipated—I had a big smile on my face (though there'd been tears in my eyes when the fear was moved by my attitude.)*

Surprisingly, scientific studies have shown that an emotion only lasts thirty seconds in the body. However, most of us do not give enough attention to the feeling at the moment it's being experienced—particularly if it's an uncomfortable one. Instead, we tend to think about what's happened, analyse, consider what to say or do next—and some 'lose it' and lash out. For over thirty years I've been an advocate of the saying 'The fastest way to freedom is to feel your feelings'. But putting it into practice is still a work in progress for me.

Failure to release emotions can lead to ill health. If we don't really feel an emotion and allow it to go of its own accord, that emotion will keep coming back until we do— or until we die. Unfelt feelings of anger, resentment or guilt build up over time and are easily triggered by something or someone they're not really about. Most of us have a store of unfelt emotional energy stuck in our bodies, and we can react out of all proportion to a tiny trigger.

These days we are often advised not to take it personally if someone upsets us. We might be aware that the one behaving badly is in pain and we might even come to have compassion for them. But the behaviour of others can't trigger an emotional response in us unless we already have that energy stuck in our body.

So, ideally, we might even feel gratitude that the other person has given us an opportunity to feel and let go of something that's been holding us back.

As babies we naturally express ourselves by making sounds—crying, screaming, gurgling, chuckling. But we soon learn to keep quiet and we lose the ability to express our emotions through sound. Some therapists consider that strong unexpressed emotions, along with our natural desire to feel better, contribute to addictions.

Today many people are feeling strong anger at what is happening in the world. There's also much fear and regret at what the future will hold for their children and grandchildren. Many feel that they cannot do anything to change the direction the world is going. I have a feeling that the widespread fear and disturbance and grief in the world today is affecting and triggering us all.

When I wrote my memoir two years ago I had no difficulty with writing every single day. Each morning after waking I started the day by sitting up in bed and writing. This year, I've frequently felt 'unsettled' and I've constantly questioned whether I needed to forget about a second book and remove any unnecessary pressure. My gut feeling was to continue. But just this morning when I was ready to write, my mind went blank. I thought of leaving it until tomorrow, then realised I could just write anything, even 'rubbish', as it's the first draft and I can change or delete it later. What then came into my mind was that I needed to take my own advice and give full attention to what I was feeling—I was feeling a lot of disappointment and frustration.

I still have difficulty actually feeling my emotions, but I closed my eyes and mentally said 'I'm feeling the disappointment' and 'I'm feeling the frustration'. As I continued—keeping my attention on the words—I began to feel strong reactions in my body. It was almost like inward crying for a short time before the feelings dissipated and left me full of peace.

I'm convinced that, at the present time in the history of mankind, feelings/emotions are being experienced more intensely and more frequently than ever before. In the past, we've had the 'Age of Reason'—maybe this era will be seen as the *Age of Feeling*—a time when we come to acknowledge and release the strong emotions that are preventing us from being completely loving and peaceful.

Emotions and accidents

There are many common expressions like 'Keep your mind on what you are doing' and 'Mind out!' I've been aware for many years now that it's when my mind wanders onto something that brings up so-called 'negative' emotions and judgement that I have accidents. And the severity of the accident seems to be related to the intensity of those thoughts and feelings. A momentary digression can result in a small cut or a slight burn.

The first time I became aware of this connection was on the occasion of a fairly serious car accident. It was the day Baghdad fell (9 April, 2003), with the symbolic and powerful toppling of the statue of the president, Saddam Hussein—a man portrayed to us as evil and supportive of 'terror'. Earlier in the year, the US had invaded Iraq to depose Saddam and put an end to his regime.

I was listening to the live report on my car radio as I drove from my home in the Blue Mountains to pick up one of my sons from Sydney Airport. My youngest son was beside me in the car and I was making judgemental comments on what I was hearing. The road was icy and slippery. I was at a sharp bend in the road and was 'full of bad feeling' towards Saddam Hussein. The car slid and I totally lost control. I knew that applying the brakes could make things worse, but I had no idea what I needed to do and my mind was blank as we headed for the railing between the road and a sheer drop into the valley below. Fortunately, for both of us, we didn't go through that railing. It was as if invisible hands had taken control of the steering wheel. My car did connect with the strong metal railing and was badly damaged, and we didn't get to the airport—but neither of us was injured.

* * *

How can you experience more joy in regard to your emotions?

Basically, the answer is to just feel whatever feeling arises when it arises. It may be that you need to go to the bathroom to sit quietly if you experience a strong and unpleasant emotion when you're with other people. It certainly helps to keep your mouth shut at these times and not to think about what or who triggered the emotion. Make sure you take time to feel it fully as soon as you have the opportunity. Hopefully, in time, all the unpleasant feelings will have been released and there'll be no need for you to have more of those experiences.

In the case of grief and major loss, be especially kind to yourself and let go of any judgement in regard to your grieving behaviour. Some of us seem to carry on as if nothing has happened, while others can hardly function, and some can't stop talking. But do make sure you give attention to the actual feeling within.

2. MESSAGES FROM THE BODY

It is through our tactile sense (touch) that we experience our own physical bodies. Sensations and signals are constantly being generated and sent to the brain. These messages from the body have little to do with the outside world, but our awareness of them and our reactions (or non-reactions) definitely affect the way we *are*—and thus the vibes coming from us. They have no audible sound, smell, taste or touch. There is nothing we can see. They are not emotions, though they may trigger emotions.

I'm referring to signals such as feeling hot or cold regardless of the outside temperature, feeling nausea, the signals of a full bladder or need for a bowel movement, feeling the need to lie down or sit or stand or stretch.

It's important to remember that everything we experience with our eyes, nose, mouth, ears and touch is giving us information to keep us safe and functioning well. It really is essential for our well-being that we learn to take notice of all these sensations/signals, and respond appropriately.

The value of tiredness, discomfort and pain

It's our tactile sense that notifies the brain when we are in need of rest and healing. The sensation of *tiredness* usually comes first, but is commonly ignored. There are options of eating or drinking something stimulating or of pushing on regardless. But if we do that, we are not addressing the problem. Our body needs rest, and for our well-being we need to stop what we've been doing as soon as we can.

If we ignore tiredness, discomfort will follow. If that is ignored, we get pain. Pain is an important 'felt' sensation. It certainly doesn't bring immediate joy, but it is a major sign that all is not well and that there's a need to stop and make appropriate changes before further damage is done. We naturally pull our hand away from a hot iron if we touch it accidentally. We do not keep our hand there and take a 'pain-killer' to prevent our brain from getting the message being sent. Yet it seems common practice to disregard or 'silence' signals of discomfort, disorder and even pain in our physical bodies. Most of us tend to ignore them until an accident or severe illness stops us in our tracks and enforces rest. And then it's often too late to return to the status quo/former good health.

Self-care is often well down our list of priorities. Commercial interests persuade us to spend lots of our money on what is offered in the guise of self-care. Gym equipment, devices to measure our heartbeats or footsteps, food 'supplements', products to relax us, to stimulate us, to put on our skin, to colour our hair, to help us lose weight— even surgery for purely cosmetic reasons might be regarded as self-care. But a relaxing bath and an early night or a device-free day (essential use only) or a day at the beach or in a forest/bushland would, in my opinion, be more nurturing and beneficial.

Conversations with the body

One of the most unusual and interesting books I've ever read was written by a woman who needed a heart transplant and was advised to 'talk to her heart'. *When the Heart Speaks, Listen,* by Lerita Coleman Brown, Ph.D., is described as 'a unique biological thriller with valuable psychological and spiritual insights'. The author records months of conversations with both her old heart and the new one she eventually received. Her ability to connect to its wisdom and guidance absolutely transformed her life. It's an eye-opening book, and I enjoyed it very much. I had read before of people who'd had conversations with organs in their bodies that were not functioning well. They'd all written about the healing that took place as a result.

***

How can you experience more joy from your body's messages?

Keep in mind that all the signals from your physical body are for your benefit. So, as soon as is possible, get more rest if you feel tired and do what you know is best for *your* body in regard to food, drink and general self-care.

Notice and respond appropriately to all of your body's signals—and definitely do not ignore pain. Take time, regularly, to be completely still and scan your body from toes up, noting any tension. Tension can always be detected and it's easy to then relax that part, whether it's jaw, shoulders, feet or whatever.

Look at your physical body with awe, wonder and respect. Focus on all the things it's doing so well. It is an amazing creation. You might even decide to 'talk' to parts of it and get to know it better!

3. BREATH

I wasn't sure where to place this topic, but since breathing depends on the movement of lungs, muscles etc, it can definitely be classified as tactile.

Breath can be *felt* —when it is inhaled through our nostrils, when it is exhaled onto a hand held in front of the mouth, and when it fills our lungs and belly.

Breath can be *seen*—when the outside air is cold, and when our breath causes our chest, belly, our clothing or bedclothes to move.

Breath can be *heard*—when it is exhaled through the mouth, when there's any obstruction (noisy breathy, snoring), when we are excited (heavy breathing) or short of breath (panting).

Historically, breath has been considered in terms of the concept of life force. Spirit, prana, psyche and similar words relate to this concept of breath. In the Bible, God breathed life into clay to make Adam a living soul.

Inhalation is essential for bringing oxygen into the body for what is called 'cellular respiration', and the ensuing act of exhalation releases waste in the form of carbon dioxide. But breathing has other important functions. It provides a mechanism for speech, singing, humming, laughter and other expressions of emotion. It's also used for reflexes such as yawning, coughing or sneezing. And, of course, it allows us to experience smell.

When we breathe, we inhale and exhale breath—the air around us. It is something we do automatically from birth to death. Some say that during our lives we take a fixed number of breaths, and so the more slowly we breathe, the longer we live. Whether or not there is any truth in that statement, we do have the ability to notice and make changes to our breathing.

We can alter the length of our breath at each step, holding it before exhaling, waiting before breathing in again. We can visualise it travelling to a certain part of the body or wrapping around us. We can attach colour to it. We can breathe through alternate nostrils, in and out of the nose, in and out of the mouth, or a mixture of both. All of these affect the way our bodies function. You are probably aware that deliberately taking slow, deep breaths can help us relax when nervous or upset, as does the quick 'blowing out' I've sometimes noticed contestants doing in TV quizzes.

Some of us, in preparing for childbirth, have practiced several ways of breathing and learned to switch from one to another in order to best cope with each stage of the birth process.

About fifty years ago I needed to spend two nights in a hospital following a miscarriage. The first night, the other women in my ward were restless and unable to get to sleep. They not only talked most of the time—at 2 a.m. some of them lit up cigarettes and smoked as they continued to chat in the dark. As a former smoker I found this most unpleasant and undesirable. So on night two, as soon as the lights were out I suggested we all do some relaxing breathing, and I led them in a taking twelve very slow, deep breaths. I think they were all asleep before I finished, as there wasn't another sound in the ward until the next day.

I'm aware that these days there are apps we can download for our phones or other devices to assist us in specific breathing practices. One I've looked at, *Breathe +,* is described as 'a beautifully simple way to visualise your breathing' and it's designed for everyday relaxation. The guided sessions last from one minute to one hour and the settings allow the user to adjust the length of inhalation, exhalation and holds.

Specific kinds of breathing are used in Tai Chi, yoga and many forms of meditation. Since its invention in the 1950s, the Buteyko breathing method has been taught to many asthmatics and people with breathing-related issues, e.g. sleep apnoea and snoring. The courses provide training in correct breathing and have been extremely successful.

An unusual but very ancient breathing technique is used by some players of wind instruments. It is called 'circular breathing' and it's something I'd planned to learn a few years ago after buying a Jew's Harp. The player breathes in and out at the same time in order to produce a continuous sound. Air is drawn into the nostrils while it is simultaneously being blown into the instrument (using air stored in the cheeks). Many traditional instrumentalists, including didgeridoo and mouth-harp players and some classical and jazz players, use this method today. I believe the record length of time for producing one continuous sound is fifty minutes.

***

How can you experience more joy through breathing?

Begin to take notice of your breath. If you don't already do regular deep breathing, then try it out in whatever form appeals to you. Evidently, most of us do not breathe deeply, automatically. Just three deep breaths before *any* activity can be of enormous benefit. Certainly, if feeling anxious, slow and deep breathing is the best 'go to'.

Certain breathing patterns will occur naturally according to your mood. But you can actually change a mood to a more comfortable one by focusing on the breath and changing its pattern. You might visualise the air coming into your nostrils as being of a particular colour or as white light—whatever comes to mind. You could allow that air to travel down to the abdominal area, noticing the belly swell and deflate with each breath. Then imagine that each part, each cell, of your physical body is relaxing and opening up to the healing properties of the breath/colour/energy continually coming in. You could then quickly scan the whole body and notice any tension, then direct the next breath to that part to allow it to relax completely…

So often, when we are not feeling great, we analyse and think about the way we are, and we want to change. We might try to comfort ourselves with food, drink or distractions. If we're with a partner or someone else close to us we want them to 'bring us out of it' by saying or doing something helpful. From my experience, it doesn't work that way. No matter how loving or willing the other person is, they can't 'fix us'. But we can use that first gift we ever received—the breath. It can be a magical solution.

CHAPTER 8

Taste

Taste, also known as the gustation, is what we experience when we put something in our mouth. Babies and children instinctively put everything into their mouths as they investigate the world around them. Taste gives us information about both harmful and beneficial things—the bitterness of poisons and the sweetness of energy-rich foods.

The mechanics of taste

There is a *chemical* reaction when a substance in the mouth reacts with the taste receptor cells located in the pores (papillae) on the tongue, on the roof, sides and back of the mouth, and in the throat and lungs. There are thousands of these pores each containing up to 100 receptor cells. As we eat, saliva, with its digestive enzymes, begins to dissolve the food, washing the chemicals over the papillae. The receptor cells then generate nerve impulses (taste signals), which send information to the brain.

Taste signals are also sent by nerves to the nasal cavity (where they can cause the nose to drip), and to the lacrimal gland (where they may make the eyes water or produce tears). A hot curry will do that to me. Scientists used to believe that there were regions on the tongue dedicated to each of the basic tastes, but current research indicates that all of the tastes can be detected at any point on the tongue.

As soon as our brain receives the gustatory signals, connections from the lower brain influence our digestive processes, triggering the release of seratonin (the 'happiness' hormone) during and after a meal. The salivary nuclei are also signalled to decrease saliva production when we've satisfied our hunger. I find that interesting, as I've recently had two experiences of difficulty swallowing towards the end of a large meal. It happened yesterday, and my sense was that there wasn't enough saliva. I know I'd eaten too much. I was eating a take-away meal with a visitor.

The saying 'too much of a good thing' really is true in regard to food. It can be tempting to have more of something pleasurable, but doing so doesn't usually result in more pleasure. Quite the opposite. I used to think my grandmother was strange when she said we should leave the table feeling we could eat more. But I see the wisdom of her words now.

Smell and taste

It's been said that between 75 and 95 percent of what we think of as taste actually comes from the sense of smell— the other chemical sense. Taste and smell work together as they allow tiny molecules from the outside world into our bodies and bind to them. What we commonly call the taste of food or beverage is actually a multisensory phenomenon. The sense of taste gives basic information about sweet, sour, bitter and so on, but most of the food experience depends on the sense of smell. And additional senses are involved in perceiving the texture and temperature of everything that goes into our mouth.

When we chew food or sip wine, chemicals are vaporised into air passages that connect the mouth and the back of the nose, stimulating olfactory (smell) receptors and allowing us to realise the subtleties of flavour. Taste plus smell equals flavour.

We can become aware of how smell affects flavour by plugging our nose while eating—it results in a significant decrease in flavour. Conversely, we get more flavour out of our food by chewing slowly. That way more of its aroma can be detected in the nose. Artificial fragrances, as well as flavours, are nowadays added to many foods.

I find it mind-boggling that our body cells are completely replaced on a regular basis, but *every week* new taste buds replace old ones to keep our sense of taste sharp.

The basic tastes

Taste perception is unique to each of us, but the way of categorising tastes has been standardised. It is generally considered that there are five basic tastes sensed by our taste buds and sent to the brain—*sweet, salty, sour, bitter and umami*. The last taste, umami, comes from the

Japanese word for 'savoury' (some say it means 'deliciousness'). Umami tastes come from foods like broth and meat. In 2015 researchers suggested adding a new basic taste, *fat taste*—oleogustus or pinguis were the proposed names for it.

The first known classification of basic tastes was way back in 350 BC, when Aristotle postulated that the most basic tastes were sweet and bitter. In ancient China, spiciness was a category. In the ancient Indian healing science of Ayurveda the traditional basic tastes are sweet, salty, sour, bitter, pungent and astringent.

Reduction in taste perception

Scientists say that as we age, there is a decline in the number of tongue papillae. Certainly, loss of teeth or the wearing of dentures can affect the quality of chewing and the breaking down of food particles. Saliva secretion can also decline as a result of ageing, so less liquid is available to help the food compounds dissolve. General health, medications, infections and environmental factors can all play a part. However, it's also said that a healthy diet, active lifestyle and low to moderate consumption of food can help slow down the changes in papillae. I have dentures covering the roof of my mouth, but at age eighty-seven I enjoy the taste of my food at least as much as I did when I was young.

Some taste terminology

An *innate taste* refers to tastes that are enjoyable to most people when they first experience them.

An *acquired taste* is quite the opposite. We may need substantial exposure before finding the taste enjoyable. It could be because of its smell (durian), taste (the bitterness of coffee and Brussels sprouts), mouthfeel (the sliminess of oysters), appearance (insects) or association (blood sausage).

Aftertaste is the taste we experience after food or drink has left the mouth—either swallowed or spat out.

Food craving is a selective hunger for a food or non-food item. Studies on food cravings seem to indicate that cravings are *not related to missing nutrients,* vitamins or minerals. Most craving is for foods with high levels of sugar glucose. It's not really surprising in a society where sweets and sweet foods are regarded as 'treats' or rewards. In addition, sugar is addictive, as when the glucose interacts with the opioid receptor system in the brain, an addictive triggering effect occurs.

Tea tasting

Tea tasting is done by trained testers who can detect the different tastes in teas due to varying climatic conditions, topography, manufacturing process and different cultivars of the plant. Using a large spoon, they noisily slurp the liquid into their mouth so that both the tea and plenty of oxygen pass over their tongue's taste receptors. The liquid is then expelled into a spittoon.

Wine tasting

For many people, a wine tasting is an enjoyable event. The activity is as old as the history of wine, though the word 'tasting' first appeared in 1519. The methodology was formalised by the eighteenth century, the stages being: appearance, aroma, in-mouth sensations and the 'finish' (aftertaste). A significant part of the pleasure of the wine tastings I've attended has been the relaxed and friendly atmosphere, the expectation of having an enjoyable time, and no time pressure. It's interesting that in a well-publicised double-blind taste test in 2011 (in Hertfordshire, England, and involving members of the public) the 400 participants could not tell the difference between cheap and expensive wine.

Locavore

Locavore was the word of the year for 2007 in the Oxford American Dictionary. The term locavore was coined by a group of women in San Francisco, who encouraged people to eat locally produced food (within a 100-mile radius of where they lived). Locavores reject the idea that any food should be available anywhere, at any time of the year, as locally grown is fresher and it helps local growers.

I remember being recommended to eat locally grown, seasonal produce for its health benefits back in the 1960s.

Digital lollipop

This is an electronic device which stimulates the tongue with electric currents, simulating sweet, sour, salty and bitter tastes. It also produces varying amounts of heat to simulate food. The digital lollipop was developed at the National University of Singapore. It's said that eventually it could be used to help Alzheimer's patients and diabetics.

Ways we eat and drink

While we may occasionally find ourselves attending wine tastings or cheese tastings, the majority of our taste experiences are from our daily consumption of food and drinks.

But what an extreme! From taking time at a wine tasting to enjoy and analyse the smell before moving a tiny amount around in the mouth while focusing on the flavour—to the rushed eating and drinking so many people do these days.

Life can be so busy that, for some, it's become a habit to eat on the move. And certainly, many people drink coffee and similar drinks on the go. Gone are the days when most families began their meals quietly sitting around the meal table, leaving behind thoughts of past and future as they joined in silence to give thanks and ask blessing on the food before them. In my mother's day, children were literally 'seen but not heard' at mealtimes. Today, it's normal for the TV to be on, and distracting smart phones nearby. It's quite likely that the family members are not together at the table. Eating tends to be combined with other activities, with time seeming to be at a premium.

Two years ago, my Facebook friend Emily Regina Hsu published a small book on mindful eating. Emily is a Chinese American, and she wrote of her path from cancer and poor health to regaining inner peace, joy, love and hope. She said that a lot of research has been done on the benefits of mindful eating. Eating slowly and chewing thoroughly makes us more relaxed, turns off stress and turns on digestion. (Stress triggers the body to shut down digestion.) Emily states that eating when stressed leads to the food being stored as fat instead of being digested. This can result in fat accumulation in the belly, issues with digestion and absorption, thyroid problems and metabolism problems.

Her recommendations include:

Considering the atmosphere—a serene setting without TV, computers or any devices or other distractions

Taking three deep breaths before eating—holding the in-breaths before releasing them

Expressing gratitude

Smiling when eating and swallowing

Chewing each mouthful 20-30 times (putting down cutlery while chewing)

Aim for 80 percent satisfied, not full

I was brought up to chew rice or other starchy foods thirty times, as carbohydrate digestion is begun by the saliva in the mouth. I've been able to comfortably follow all of Emily's suggestions apart from the first one—playing Upwords on my iPad at mealtimes when I am alone. (Though since my little dopamine detox, I'm happy to look out the window instead. Or, if I'm eating outside, I'm happy just to watch the clouds or the birds in nearby trees.)

Conflicting advice on what to eat and drink

Many people are saying that the time has come for us to let go of all the 'old stories'—the old beliefs, the analysis. In my opinion, nowhere is this more relevant than in regard to what we taste—our choice of food and drink. For many years we have been bombarded with advice on what we should or shouldn't eat and drink. And much of it is contradictory and confusing, and achieves quite the opposite to 'sparking joy'.

How much water do we need?

I studied 'natural health' back in the 1960s, and was taught to drink water if and when thirsty, and never with a meal or close to one, since water with food interfered with the digestive process. I followed this advice until early last year when I became extremely ill. A close friend whose opinion I value, and the medical intuitive I consulted, told me that I needed to drink more water—six to eight glasses every day. I made the decision to follow their advice. I was well aware of the current recommendations by health professionals, dieticians and others to drink lots of water.

For over a year I drank as much water as I could get down. It was still less than recommended, as I chose not to drink with meals. I had to force myself to drink it, almost gagging at times, but I wanted to do what I believed was the right thing.

Early this year I read a book on self-healing by R J Spina, which stated that 'constant hydration actually depletes the body of essential electrolytes and minerals through urination'. I stopped forcing myself to drink water and let thirst be my guide. It was like a burden being lifted. (With hindsight, I probably was dehydrated when I became ill, as I'd had most of my teeth out, and even after I was wearing dentures, it was hard work chewing some fruits and any raw vegetables; I was definitely consuming much less water in my food at the time.) I was even more delighted a few days ago when I read a book by Natalia Rose, a top nutritionist in the USA and much sought after by models, actors, socialites and media personalities. She recommends a hydrating diet of fresh fruits and vegetables and homemade green juices, 'leaving the cells with little or no water requirements'. She also advised against drinking with meals, apart from sipping wine.

Dairy products

The dairy industry and many of today's dieticians want us to believe that milk/milk products from cows is necessary for calcium for our bones. All milk is produced naturally for the young of the species and is the perfect food for them. But once animals have teeth and can feed themselves, they normally cease drinking their mother's milk. Leafy greens contain calcium along with the magnesium needed for it to be absorbed, in perfect ratio. Pasteurised dairy intake is linked to thyroid conditions and diabetes, and can block iron absorption, according to Natalia Rose (and many others). There are numerous studies that claim that adult humans should avoid cow's milk and dairy products.

It can all be so confusing. And 'experts' who give advice or release reports are often in the pay of those with vested interests.

Choosing what we eat and drink

I doubt that anyone reading these words forages for food as early man did. Some 'primitive' tribes might still be selecting their food by tasting the plants that are growing nearby and checking the flesh of fish or animal for freshness before eating, but I imagine none of us is using our sense of taste to determine what we put into our mouths to eat or drink. With a foodstuff we've never tried we might taste it before making the decision to eat it, and if the sensation is unpleasant 'spit it out'.

Today, in much of the world, the first meal of the day that breaks our overnight fast may consist of coffee or tea or juice, toast and/or cereal with milk. Or it might be a green smoothie, eggs, fresh fruits, yoghurt, cheese, waffles, croissants, pancakes, bagels, French toast, sausages, kedgeree or porridge. I remember what a vast array of breakfast dishes were available in the buffets on the cruise ships prior to the pandemic.

It seems that the decisions about what we eat are very much based on habit—the way our families ate—or our beliefs. Our sense of taste is not what usually determines our food choices. Maybe we eat what someone else has prepared. We might read or somehow hear from others that a foodstuff is good for us or helps with excess weight… and so we make a change.

Powerful manufacturers spend a lot of money advertising their products (which we are probably better *not* eating/drinking). I've always thought if something needs to be advertised, it can't be beneficial. Word of mouth would do all the advertising necessary for a product that would benefit *us* rather than the manufacturer.

Our society has strong views on what are desirable or not desirable foods. I disagree with many of them—for I believe they stem from vested interests. Fortunately, the experts agree that fruits and vegetables (especially green leafy vegetables), nuts, seeds and whole grains— in other words 'plants'—are beneficial. Actually, I was surprised back in the 1960s when my foster daughter was studying biology to read in her text book that the *necessary food for humans is plants*—either directly or by eating animals that have eaten plants. I'd never before come across the theory that people eat meat in order to get the benefit of the plants those animals have eaten.

Cacao

This raw, less-processed version of cocoa, is the purest form of chocolate and has become very popular in recent years. However, there's evidence that as early as 460 AD African tribes used it to tap into higher mental and physical highs, and even solve problems more clearly and confidently. Cacao became the Mayan form of money. It was brought to the 'New World' by Christopher Columbus. There are said to be vaults of raw cacao buried all over the world.

In 1519 Hernando Cortes, the Spanish conquistador, described the hot cacao drink as 'the divine drink which builds up resistance and fights fatigue. A cup of this precious drink permits a man to walk for a whole day without food'.

Raw cacao contains a chemical called 'anandamide'— taken from the Sanskrit word for bliss, happiness, pleasure, joy and delight. Black truffle mushrooms are the only other known food with a significant enough amount of this 'bliss chemical' per serving to have a noticeable effect on our mood.

Cacao also stimulates the release of several feel-good hormones, including oxytocin, which promotes happiness and a sense of well-being. It is packed with essential vitamins and nutrients (including magnesium, iron and calcium) and has been shown to lower blood pressure, improve blood flow to the brain and heart, and aid in preventing blood clots. It is, indeed, a superfood. I'm most grateful that I can order top-quality cacao from my supermarket. I mix it with freshly ground almonds and sunflower seeds and cinnamon, and have three heaped spoonfuls on my breakfast bowl each day.

***

What do you taste that makes you joyful?

How can you take stock of what you are currently experiencing through your sense of taste? How can you determine which of your foods and drinks really brings joy? At your next meal, see if you can identify each of the five tastes as you eat. You'll gain a new appreciation for your brain and how hard it works.

More importantly, I suggest that whenever possible for the next week or so, you make a note of whatever food and drink (apart from water) you put in your mouth, and record beside each item whether or not you actually enjoyed it. If you are considering changing your taste experiences to ones that produce more joy, it can also be helpful to notice your responses before and after the items are eaten or drunk. I did this for several days and found it most worthwhile.

The last time I ate out at a restaurant I was amazed at how delicious the first mouthfuls of my food tasted. I was flooded with 'feel-good' hormones. The taste sensations were the strongest I've experienced in my whole life! But then what surprised me in a different way was that, after a very short time, those sensations completely changed. Switched off. I continued eating for a while, but the pleasure had gone. I was less than halfway through eating what was on my plate; to have continued would have meant forcing myself to chew and swallow when my body was saying 'enough'. Fortunately I'd brought a container with me, and I packed up the remainder, took it home and really enjoyed it the next day.

Not only is it more comfortable to not overeat, but if the body's energy is being depleted unnecessarily on digestion, then it cannot be as effective at fighting illness, building immunity, and maintaining general upkeep of cells, tissues and organs. Digestion can use more energy than is derived from the food being digested.

In addition to taking stock of what you are eating, notice your thirst and liquid intake. You may choose to make some changes — in particular, cutting down or eliminating drinking water or water-based drinks with meals.

If you're preparing food, be as relaxed as possible. Prepare it with love, and present the food attractively. Consider the setting for meals, eat more quietly and mindfully, chewing each mouthful longer, savouring the flavour, relaxing and enjoying the experience. Feel gratitude for what you are eating. Focus on the tastes and texture of your food. Notice your body's responses whenever you are eating and be aware of any indication to stop.

At least for a while, why not let go of all the theories and advice of others and just pay attention to your body's signals and responses — and to which tastes bring you joy.

CHAPTER 9

Smell

Smell, or olfactory perception, is what we experience when breath comes into our nose and we sense odours or scents.

The mechanics of olfaction

As we breathe in, airborne particles enter the nose and reach little clusters of specialised receptor cells in what is called the olfactory bulb. These cells are in fact neurons—with one end in direct contact with the external world and the other in direct contact with the brain. We have four hundred or so of them sending electrical impulses to the brain which is able to compute at least ten thousand and possibly a trillion different odours.

Smell has been described as the primal sense. It is unique and powerful and is the only one of our five senses that connects to *two* areas of the brain—the regions linked with emotion and memory (the amygdala and the hippocampus).

I've read of tests carried out on people who were placed in a stressful situation while imperceptible amounts of a fragrance were diffused around them. Later, they were exposed to the same odour *without the stress,* and their bodies tended to react the same way as previously. An odour can trigger nearly instantaneous feelings of fear or desire before we are even aware of what we are smelling.

Emotionally charged memories, even nostalgia and longing can be evoked by the smells around us. There's a particular oil smell that always takes me back onboard the Danish freighter I travelled on at the age of twenty. It was a very happy time of my life, and that smell, which many might find unpleasant, always triggers joy for me.

Important functions of our sense of smell include the detection of desirable or spoiled foods, various kinds of hazards, and pheromones—those airborne particles we and other animals emit which play an essential role in sexual attraction and repulsion.

Smell also contributes greatly to our enjoyment of food. As previously mentioned, it is smell plus taste that creates what we call 'flavour'. When we eat, the data received from both tongue and nose is compiled by the brain and perceived as flavour. *Inhaling deeply over food before eating is said to make us more aware of when we're full.* Chewing slowly means more of the scent of the food can be detected in the nose—a good reason for taking our time when eating.

Even with pleasing scents, the stronger the smell, the more unpleasant and nauseating it becomes. This is something to bear in mind when we use scented products for our person or environment.

It's said that the olfactory system of a foetu
functional by twenty-five weeks, and a newborn ba
use its sense of smell to find the breast. A breastfed baby
able to recognise its mother by her odour, and at one
month of age, an article of the mother's clothing with her
natural body odour placed in the baby's crib will help the
little one settle and go to sleep. The smell of an item from
its mother can bring comfort to a baby or child in the event
of separation, e.g. if one of them is hospitalised.

Smells that repel

Certain smells are known to repel. We can use aromas as
repellents on ourselves, in the garden and on our pets.
There are natural smells that repel birds, cats, dogs, mice,
ants, spiders and roaches, as well as biting insects such as
mosquitos. Fortunately, today, many pest exterminators
are using eco-friendly, nontoxic natural scents to rid our
homes of unwanted visitors.

I know from personal experience that body odour can be a
complete turnoff, but I found it interesting to learn that
research has indicated that the scent of *female tears*
apparently dampens male sexual desire. I had the
impression that a woman crying didn't bring out the best
in most men—but now perhaps we know why! Fear and
certain illnesses alter body odour, and it's thought that
happiness may also release a particular odour in our
perspiration.

Smells that give warning

Physical discomfort is a most important communication from the body, and an unpleasant smell can be a message to us that we need to take action, by either removing ourselves from the situation or by making some other change in our behaviour.

Can we change our perception of a smell?

Occasionally, we may be stuck with an unpleasant smell, whether we like it or not—such as in a packed train close to a person who has just farted, has strong body odour or is wearing strong perfume. Perhaps we can change our experience of such a smell by focusing our full attention on it and not engaging our minds/thoughts. I suggest this, despite not having tried it. I know it can work with sound and sight and I have a feeling that with any of our 'five senses' we have the ability to consciously influence our experiences.

Colour-coded sensory maps feature smell

Students from the University of Technology in Sydney have this year been recording the Saturday-night 'stinks of cigarettes and alcohol and people going out' and the Sunday morning 'smell of coffee or salty sweat from people jogging'. They have mapped several suburbs according to smell, touch, sound, taste and sight. It is thought that the sensory maps they've produced will be of particular interest to both planners and visitors to the city.

Forest bathing

I discovered recently that the smell of mycobacterium vacii, a micro-organism found in soil, compost and leaf mould, triggers the release of serotonin (the mood-lifting hormone). What is nowadays called 'forest bathing' provides an opportunity for us to breathe in these 'scents' along with the essential oils from the trees. Of particular benefit is the smell of fir or pine trees. I'm lucky that my route to the nearest shopping centre takes me past a hidden-away park surrounded by trees and shrubs and deep in leaf mulch. I'm always struck by the strong and enjoyable smell as I walk past that area.

It's recommended that we experience 'proper' forest bathing once a month—listening to the sounds, looking around at the natural beauty, maybe feeling the sun on our body, breathing in the fresh air away from toxicity as we engage most/all of our senses. It's a perfect place for meditation and stillness, and an opportunity to recharge and nurture ourselves—in mind, body and spirit.

The fragrance of flowers

'Stop and smell the flowers' is an often-used expression reminding us to relax, enjoy and appreciate the beauty of life. There is a most wonderfully perfumed white rose inside one of the entrances to the retirement village where I live. It is at its best right now, and I make a point of stopping and putting my face close to the flower as I pass — experiencing the pleasure and joy it brings. And the experience is free! We need to keep in mind that the best things in life *are* free and available to us when we stop our busyness and striving for what we think will bring happiness, and nourish ourselves by opting for what pleases our senses.

Essential oils and incense

Essential oils are produced by vapour distillation or cold pressing of plants. They are extracted directly from *bark, leaves, roots, nuts, resins, fruit and flowers.* The Egyptians used essential oils back in 4500 BC, and anointing with oil and the use of incense has been enjoyed since the beginning of recorded history. Anointing and aromatherapy massage have the added benefits of the fragrant oil being absorbed into the body and the soothing touch on the skin, both of which increase the enjoyment and benefits as they trigger the brain to release even more of the 'feel-good' hormones.

Essential oils have been used *medicinally* for thousands of years. According to passionate aromatherapist and public health researcher, Dr Eric Zielinski, their true power is that *they help the body achieve the inner balance it needs to heal itself.* They can also have a preventative effect. Dr

Z (as he's known) has dedicated himself to spreading research-backed information on essential oils, and educating families on ways to use them to manage their own health—to get a better night's sleep, reduce stress, clear brain fog, balance hormones and ease pain.

Three oils shown by studies to be of particular value are lavender, bergamot and lemon essential oils. They not only prompt the release of serotonin and dopamine, they actually benefit our mental health, affecting mood conditions, memory issues and attention difficulties.

The word 'incense' means 'to burn'. Aromatic material is burnt and the smoke is inhaled. The plant materials are often combined with essential oils. Incense sticks and cones are lit directly by a flame, then fanned or blown out, leaving a glowing ember that smoulders and releases a smoky fragrance. I made the mistake recently of lighting a stick of Palo Santo wood (a 'cousin' of both frankincense and myrrh) right under a smoke detector. I'd been using it each morning before working on this book. After blowing out the flame and spreading the smoke around the room, I checked that the wood was no longer burning and sat at the computer ready to begin. Being in a room at the very back of my apartment and with the door closed (and being hard of hearing), I was totally unaware that the alarm outside my front door had alerted the whole retirement village and the fire brigade. Two people from the office came and asked me to open all the doors and windows in order to stop the alarm ringing. Shortly afterwards, three professional firefighters dressed up for a major blaze arrived and checked my little incense stick! It certainly brought about a change of energy for me that morning.

Smoking

The inhaling of the fumes of burning plant material is not confined to incense and fragrant wood. The inhalation through smoking of marijuana, hashish and tobacco is widespread—tobacco being legal and the most popular. It's believed the practice of smoking tobacco began as early as 5000–3000 BC.

Tobacco is a plant with a high level of nicotine. The leaves are cured, aged, then processed in a variety of ways to produce products for smoking (cigarettes, cigars and pipes), inhaling (snuff) or applying to the gums (chewing tobacco). In earlier times, smokers no doubt rolled the shredded leaves in a natural wrapper. Today, however, a cigarette has approximately six hundred ingredients and the fumes contain about seventy toxic substances considered cancer-forming. Cigarette smoke contains arsenic, acetone, ammonia, butane, cadmium, carbon monoxide, formaldehyde, lead, naphthalene, tar and benzene along with other substances known to be harmful. Most of the products on the market today expose the smoker to a toxic mix of over 7,000 chemicals.

When nicotine enters a person's blood stream, it triggers the release of adrenaline, increasing blood pressure, breathing and heart rate. Research has shown that it also affects the brain—enhancing focus and attention, improving working memory and speeding up reaction times. Cigarette smoke releases endorphins and dopamine, bringing lots of 'good feelings'. But nicotine is addictive, and while it seems to help people relax, smoking actually increases anxiety and tension and can lead to depression. Being a stimulant, it can also mask the body's signals of tiredness and disturb sleep.

Choice of 'scents' for the home

Every day I deliberately choose scents I enjoy. As well as incense, I might use essential oils in a diffuser or oil burner or on a little beaded bracelet. There are now some good-quality essential oils available in our supermarkets, and I stock up when they're on special. I've recently come across roll-on applicators filled with essential oils. They are designed for application to wrists, temples or behind the ears, and are lovely to use. I keep a small selection of essential oils in my bathroom cupboard and, at the start of the day, I sometimes put a couple of drops of one of them onto the floor of the shower (near the wall) where the water will hit it and release the fragrance. Peppermint is my favourite in the morning.

I have lavender bags, made by a friend, with my stored clothing and bedding; and just before I get into bed at night I like to use a pure lavender spray in the room and on my pillow. Yesterday, I unintentionally bought a can of a different brand of lavender spray and noticed that it suggested directing it onto the neck and shoulders before bed and, preferably, massaging it into the skin. I've not tried that yet.

Smells that sell a house

Traditionally, the recommendation has been to bake some bread in the oven before would-be buyers arrive, cook oranges with cloves or apples with cinnamon on the stovetop, or brew a pot of fresh coffee. More professional advice is to open the windows ahead of time to let stale air out and fresh air in, and ensure there are no smelly shoes near the door and that bins, pet beds and litter trays are clean. Musty furniture or furnishings are things we need to pay attention to at all times. Artificially fragranced air-fresheners should *not* be used when someone is visiting, but the empty containers can be filled with water and essential oils and used without the toxic synthetic materials. Vanilla essence in a heatproof bowl with some water, on low heat in the oven, will permeate the house with a sweet smell.

Carpets can be cleaned ahead of a sales inspection (or at any time) by sprinkling bi-carb soda mixed with essential oil, leaving it for an hour, and then vacuuming. Bi-carb in an open jar will absorb stale smells in cupboards or rooms. Houseplants help purify a room, and cut flowers such as roses, freesias, jonquils and gardenias will add both beauty and fragrance.

The use of artificial perfumes

I've never been able to wear perfumes, as such. I'm even allergic to very strong natural scents — no freesias in my rooms. On my wedding day, the driver of the car taking me to the church had to stop and put my bouquet of flowers into the boot of the car, as I was starting to wheeze. Being extremely sensitive to artificial perfumes it's essential I choose unscented everyday items. No scented toilet paper, shampoo, soap or laundry products for me. Actually, when I think about it, there are dozens of everyday items to which artificial perfumes have been added. Clearly the manufacturers and marketers are aware of the impact of scents, their effect on our emotions and their ability to remind us of happy times.

A book I highly recommend is Scent and Soul by Rohanna Goodwin Smith. I found it a beautifully written, easy to read, and most informative book. I learned a lot and I thank my lucky stars for my extreme reaction to all artificial scents and additives. Natural aromas are not harmful, but there are a surprising number of toxic chemicals in the majority of artificially scented products. Some products are heavily scented in order to cover up offensive-smelling ingredients.

An astronomical amount of money has gone into research on the psychological effects of synthetic chemical odours, despite proof that their aromatic molecules can adversely affect both the endocrine and nervous systems, provoking allergies that can lead to asthma. The close relationship between big business and government means that many existing regulations are not being enforced, and there's little incentive to bring in new regulations.

I was amazed to read of the ways large companies use scents (always the artificial ones) to *subliminally* influence people's emotions and behaviour. These fragrances are not even detectable—and they are used in many countries, in factories, casinos, stores, offices and showrooms, at sporting and political events and in all kinds of public spaces. They are even used for brochures, business cards and receipts. Hotels, motels, cruise ships, airports and public transport are all fragranced by specially chosen scents. Evidently, one of the Trump hotels had a caviar and champagne fragrance to welcome those who walk into its foyer.

Smelling salts

Used as a medicinal tool since the thirteenth century, smelling salts traditionally release ammonia gas. If someone has fainted, the sharp smell can bring them around if a bottle of smelling salts is held under their nose. If the bottle is held too close, burning may occur. The ammonia fumes irritate the interior of the nose and lungs, causing the person to take a deep breath to clear the nasal passage.

Smelling salts were very popular when I was young. Every Christmas my mother bought smelling salts for me to give to each of my school teachers (nuns). I think there were added herbs or perfumes in the beautiful little bottles. During World War II, the use of smelling salts was widely recommended and all workplaces were advised to have them in their first-aid boxes.

At the present time, Mackenzies Smelling Salts (eucalyptus and ammonia) are on the market as a traditional remedy for catarrh and head cold—reviewers also recommend it for headaches, sinus and migraine. I noticed in the online ads that strong smelling salts are used by weightlifters for a shock to the system just before lifting a heavy weight. There seems to be very mixed advice on using them that way.

Our attitude affects our sense of smell

Shakespeare's famous words 'A rose by any other name (word) would smell as sweet' imply that a sweet-smelling rose would always be sensed as sweet-smelling, regardless. But, in fact, *our attitude towards both pleasant and unpleasant smells makes a world of difference to how we perceive and experience them.* It usually takes no effort on a mother's part to deal with the dirty nappy of her baby, with its smell that others would probably find most unpleasant. I've dealt with my child's vomit without any discomfort, yet when on a boat in Greece where several people close to me were seasick, the smell turned my stomach and it took much willpower not to vomit myself.

The word 'fart', meaning to break wind, is one of the oldest words in the English language. I've read that farting is used as a greeting by the Yanomami Indian tribe in South America! Most, if not all, of us are quite comfortable with the smell of hydrogen sulphide in our own farts, but the same 'rotten egg' smell emanating from others we usually find unpleasant—despite the fact that, according to recent research, that smelly gas might provide some health benefits to humans. Yes, there's actually been a lot of scientific study into farting. In 2014 the University of Exeter and the University of Texas collaborated in researching the ability of hydrogen sulphide to reduce the effects of oxidative stress on cells. There was evidence that it could be useful for lowering blood pressure, treating heart attack and stroke, improving kidney health, protecting the brain, and reducing the effects of ageing.

When it comes to general toilet smells, there are now several products on the market that claim to trap the odours in the bowl. Unlike the air fresheners and aerosols which are used after flushing and combine the unpleasant smell with synthetic fragrances—with these products you 'spray before you go'. I've not tried them, but it's another option when it comes to choosing what we smell.

Our ability to smell is said to decline with age

As I mentioned in the chapter on taste, loss of the sense of smell can make food less appealing, affect appetite and contribute to poor nutrition in the elderly. A marked decline in olfaction can be a sign of neurological disorders and sometimes occurs early in Parkinson's and Alzheimer's disease—even years before movement or cognitive problems are noticeable. Complete loss of the sense of smell, anosmia, afflicts many people. The causes are varied and sometimes unknown. I had a friend who had no ability to detect smell. He ate to survive—there was no actual enjoyment from eating. Medications and illnesses seem to be the main triggers.

***

What smells bring you joy?

A simple way to add to your enjoyment of life is by deliberately choosing the things you smell when you are at home or that you use on your person, and taking advantage of the naturally perfumed flowers and leaves of plants. You can choose those fragrances that bring joy—and avoid the harmful synthetic fragrances that have a very different impact, physically.

We all have different biochemical makeups. Traditionally, lavender is a sedative, yet for some, it acts as a stimulant, so it's definitely best to let your body be your guide. Choose what brings you joy and it will no doubt be of most benefit. Make mindful smelling a habit.

Check out the fragranced items you already have — especially in the bathroom. Consider buying unscented products in the future, or the fragrances that really bring you joy.

If you're not familiar with essential oils you might buy some and/or read about their use. Inside, you could try using myrrh, pine, sandalwood or orange oil with fir, either in a diffuser or simply by inhaling the fragrance from a cotton wool ball.

Above all, find time to enjoy nature's fragrances outside — forest bathing, walking, or just 'smelling the roses'.

CHAPTER 10

Non-Physical Sensing

I've just come across the expression 'sense with your mind'. It is the perfect way of describing those experiences we have that are not sensed by the physical body. We have the ability to visualise, imagine or see in *our mind's eye* without involving our physical eyes. For many years I worked part-time as a carer to people who were confined to their homes. I would enthusiastically talk to them about what was going on in my life and they were able to visualise clearly the incident, the movie or the book that I'd been talking about. I was able to transfer, through my words and manner, the things I'd seen with my eyes in such a way that they felt they'd been there and seen it themselves.

Visualisation and imagination

Thinking about feeling the sun's warmth on our skin can bring relaxation and other physical changes. *Visualising* biting into a lemon or eating a favourite dessert brings definite changes in our mouths. *Imagining* ourselves on holiday as we make our plans can 'feel good'. Our brain receives messages and information from the thoughts *we* send it in addition to what is physically sensed. The significant thing is that both ways of sensing can result in a similar physical reaction.

We can deliberately use our imagination to visualise a joyful sensory experience. I'd not realised before just how powerful we are in that regard, and how much control we have over what we experience and how we function. I can compensate for not being physically touched (other than by my dentist or hairdresser) by *imagining* that I'm receiving a soothing massage and by consciously feeling the bliss and relaxation that it brings.

Visualisation can use all five senses as we imagine or picture things in our minds. By regularly visualising a goal in full sensory detail, the mind can be trained to respond as if the outcome were true at the present moment. It's known that mentally practising a physical skill is very effective—a golfer, a musician or sportsman can markedly improve their performance just by 'practising' mentally (even if confined to a hospital bed).

Visualisation directs our attention and focus to what matters to us. Focusing on the goal and taking deliberate steps towards it increases the likelihood of it happening. If you are feeling nervous, visualising the desired outcome can also help by directing your attention away from the anxiety—though, obviously, good preparation is necessary for a good performance.

It is important to bear in mind that if we visualise or focus on something we don't want to happen—problems, difficulties, the worst possible scenario—then the energy we are giving it might contribute to creating the very thing we don't want. It's never helpful to focus on the problem. Our focus and attention need to be on the solution. And an attitude of gratitude always helps.

Guided meditation

A guided meditation uses imagination and visualisation to create a variety of beneficial experiences, including relaxation. There are countless helpful guided meditations available, some written and some spoken and recorded.

Prayer and visualisation

Prayer is considered more powerful if accompanied by visualisation (and gratitude). But again, we need to be careful what we pray for. When it comes to praying for individuals, I ask that they be blessed, and I might imagine them being showered with love and light. I would never pray for a specific outcome.

In April 2020 I began joining with worldwide groups that prayed at set times—the theory being that when more people do the same thing at the same time, it has extra power. These prayers were focused on those who were directly affected by the COVID virus and were either ill themselves or grieving the loss of loved ones. From the beginning I included all who were in distress—whether physically, mentally, emotionally or spiritually, and all who were grieving or fearful, and all people in positions of leadership.

At the same time I began another ritual of joining with others worldwide to visualise our planet and people in a 'perfected' state. At least once a day I have been visualising Earth as verdant and productive with clear, clean air and fresh, clean, life-giving water in the oceans, seas, rivers, even ponds. And I visualise all creatures on Earth living in health and harmony. As I do this, I'm there—in the 'Paradise'. I really feel and experience the bliss. It's a practice that lifts me and is in no way a chore. I have my phone alarm set to the worldwide 'prayer' times, and the moment it sounds I'm instantly in another place.

No-mind state—being 'in the zone'

In July this year I watched a most interesting ABC interview with former world No.1 tennis player Evonne Goolagong. She was the first Aboriginal player to grace the world stage and her grand slam wins were of particular interest to the world media. I had a personal interest in Evonne though I had never met her, as we had the same tennis coach, Vic Edwards. Mr Edwards came to our school and taught us every week during the 1940s. While Evonne wasn't even born then, I read later that she'd moved to Sydney to live with the Edwards family and that he was her coach, manager and legal guardian. Since then I've followed her progress.

In the interview, Evonne gave a detailed account of a Wimbledon final in which she was totally 'in the zone'. She said she *didn't hear anything at all* from the noisy crowd. The *ball appeared to be enormous* and easy to hit. The lines on the court looked enormous. She saw nothing but the court for the entire match, performing at the highest level with ease. How interesting that a person can not be aware of loud sounds and can visually see things so differently.

The dictionary meanings of 'in the flow' refer to being skilled, able, talented or happy. They do not indicate that special way-of-being that Evonne and many others have experienced. Terms like 'being on a roll', 'unstoppable', even 'unconscious' capture it better. Whatever terminology we use, this trancelike state, a kind of out-of-body experience, is an indication of functioning on a different brain wavelength. And it is proof that the way *we are* can make a tremendous difference to the way we experience the world.

This state of oneness and connectivity that transcends thought comes when we lose our sense of a separate self in a creative endeavour—whether it be playing sport, making or composing music, gardening, or even cooking. I realise I've experienced it many times. It's as if a higher self has taken over—and we are relaxed but energised and function at our best. At these times, whether intentionally or not, we have totally let go of the past and the future, and we are fully present.

In his book *Mind to Matter,* Dawson Church, Ph.D., refers to the 'creative trance' of a composer making music or a child at play, where they lose all awareness of the outer world as they become absorbed in their creativity. He says that their brain waves at that time are mostly in delta, with some theta and alpha, and just enough beta to function. If you are not familiar with the categories of the waves produced by the brain's electrical activity, I'll list them briefly and very generally.

Delta brain waves (.5 to 3 Hz) are the slowest recorded brain waves in humans. They are generated in deepest meditation and dreamless sleep, when external awareness is suspended and healing and regeneration are stimulated.

Theta brain waves (3 to 8 Hz) also occur during sleep and in deep meditation and, again, our senses are withdrawn from the external world and focused on signals originating from within—including intuition and information beyond our normal conscious awareness. We experience this state just before falling asleep and just before waking.

Alpha brain waves (8 to 12 Hz) are dominant in some meditative states and during quietly flowing thoughts. Alpha is the resting state of the brain, 'the power of now', being here, in the present. Alpha brainwaves aid mental coordination, calmness, alertness, mind/body integration and learning.

Beta brain waves (12 to 38 Hz) dominate our normal waking state when our attention is on the outside world. In this state, we are alert, attentive, able to make judgements and solve problems.

Gamma waves (38 to 42 Hz) are above the frequency of 'neuronal firing', so how they are generated remains a mystery. It has been speculated that these rhythms modulate perception and consciousness (which would explain some 'strange' experiences). According to brainworksneurotherapy.com researchers have discovered that gamma brain waves are highly active when we are in states of universal love, altruism, and the 'higher virtues'.

This grouping and labelling is useful, but different areas of the brain can simultaneously generate brain waves of different frequencies, and there are no distinct divisions between the different categories.

It's actually become apparent to me just this year that *everything we perceive and everything we think has an effect on the brain.* Our brains are moving, living things, with neurons firing continuously and physical changes occurring all the time in response to the signals being received. The brain controls the way the body functions. It directs the release of both 'feel-good' hormones and the ones that shut down the normal processes, creating tension and inner conflict/damage. Mindfulness, forms of meditation, and 'being in the zone' can increase focus and attention.

Extra Sensory Perception (ESP) or Sixth Sense

Now we come to the 'woo-woo' ones—those experiences and unconventional beliefs that are regarded as having little or no scientific basis. ESP is often regarded as 'paranormal ability'. Although research into various forms of ESP has been carried out for almost one hundred years, the scientific community today considers it to be pseudoscience due to the absence of an evidence base, the lack of a theory that would explain it, and the lack of positive experimental results.

However, I grew up knowing a man who learnt and practiced mental telepathy while he was a prisoner-of-war in Japan. He became able to communicate with his wife that way, and they later made a living performing on stage. I and my family have had many of the 'sixth sense' experiences mentioned below. I believe we all have the potential to perceive (or receive) a variety of non-physical sensations. ESP experiences can include, but are not limited to, the following:

Clairsentience, intuitive knowledge by feeling

Clairsentience is a *feeling* in the body—an ability to feel the vibration of other people, animals and places. It can include emotions like fear, jealousy or the physical pain or illness of others.

Clairsaliance/clairsalience, intuitive smell

Sometimes referred to as clairscent or clairscentency, it involves *smelling* a fragrance or odour of something not in one's surroundings. The smell might be of a substance, a person, a place or an animal. It is perceived without using the nose and is beyond the limitations of ordinary time and space.

Clairvoyance, intuitive vision

Clairvoyance is the ability to *see* objects, actions or future events without the use of eyes. It transcends time and space and may be a result of what is referred to as our 'third eye' or 'second sight'.

Clairaudience, intuitive hearing

Clairaudience is the ability to perceive *sounds* or words and extrasensory noise from beyond the limitations of ordinary space and time. Both my husband and my youngest sons were composers who could hear a piece of music while they were asleep, and were able to remember it after waking and write it down.

Clairgustance, intuitive taste

Clairgustance is the ability to *taste* something without actually putting it into your mouth. The perfect diet plan!

Claircognisance, intuitive knowledge or wisdom

Claircognisance is when a person has psychic *knowledge* without any physical explanation or reason. It includes pre-cognition (knowing about something before it happens) and retro-cognition (knowledge of the past—déjà vu).

Clairtangency, intuitive knowledge by touching

This is also known as psychometry. A clairtangent handles or *touches* an object or person and, in so doing, becomes aware of information about the object or its owner or its history that was not known before.

Clairtaction, intuitive touch

Clairtaction is the ability to sense *being touched* by a spiritual being or entity, and the knowing of information about that spirit.

Clairempathy, intuitive feeling of emotion

Clairempathy is the power to detect *emotional* resonances from other locations and times. The word is also used in regard to those who are extremely sensitive to the energetic vibrations of the emotions, attitudes or physical ailments of people, places or animals—the word 'empath' is often used in this context.

Claireloquence, intuitive communicating

Claireloquence is the ability to *use precisely the right word* or combination of words in order to accomplish a special objective. Channeling, automatic speaking or guided speaking is also described as claireloquence.

***

What non-physical sensing brings you joy?

You can derive much joy and benefit by using your imagination to visualise yourself having enjoyable sensory experiences. The sky is the limit, really. You might choose to be relaxing on a beach or walking through a forest inhaling the wonderful scents, observing the colours and shapes of the vegetation and listening to birdsong. You could involve memory and recall a particularly pleasing event. I frequently remember with a full heart the joy of playing the piano with my father, even though it is now close to sixty years since his death. For twenty-five years we played duets and two-piano music together and it was magical.

You could pay attention to what is in your mind when it is anticipating the future. The media seems to focus on the worst possible scenarios, but you have the choice to expect the best—or to bring your attention back to the present if you find yourself anticipating something you'd prefer not to happen. It seems to be true that when we focus our mind on anything, we somehow increase its 'energy'. Focusing our attention or thoughts on what we don't like—possible future scenarios of pain or misfortune—really affects the way our bodies function, changing our breathing, blood pressure, etc. This alters the kind of vibration/radiation from us to the rest of the world. It's a lose/lose situation. The idea of visualising what you desire has much merit.

If you are not familiar with guided meditations, you might check them out. I've noticed that there are even some 'kid-friendly' family meditations available from the Chopra website (chopra.com).

If you pray, then become aware of what you 'ask' for. Use visualisation to imagine the end result and always give thanks in advance. If anyone comes into your mind, you might respond by sending them blessings or love.

In regard to 'the Clairs', you may feel drawn to learning more about one or more of them. But notice if you do have any of those experiences. Keep an open mind. I believe many children have these abilities (imaginary friends, etc.) but they soon learn to suppress or block them.

CHAPTER 11

Chronicle

I mentioned in the introduction that my original intention was to write a chronicle on the changes triggered by the COVID-19 pandemic. Every day I had made notes on what I read or saw on television with the intention of putting it all into a book. Because my view on many aspects differs from that of the majority of people (including my family), I hope it may be of interest to read some of my observations. I present this chronicle in three sections: The Pandemic, Politics and Natural Disasters.

1. THE PANDEMIC

Since March 2020 the COVID-19 pandemic has disturbed the world and its people. While the skies and seas benefited from the cessation of flights and shipping, most of us have been facing great challenges. The unknown nature of the 'brand new' virus led to very strong reactions worldwide. Fear spread like wildfire—some said the fear was more of a threat than the virus. Life on earth changed.

Most governments quickly introduced and enforced a number of measures to 'flatten the curve'—to reduce the rapid rise in COVID cases. With no idea how long restrictions would last, there was a rush on non-perishable supermarket supplies. Toilet paper and other basic items quickly sold out everywhere as people stocked up with supplies of necessary items. Here in Australia shop shelves were mostly bare.

Some people, on returning home after essential shopping, removed all their clothing and put it straight into the washing machine, then took a shower and washed their hair and body thoroughly before changing into clean clothes. Most of us would thoroughly clean the door handle as soon as we returned from being outside. Any purchases were carefully wiped with disinfectant or put aside for some days. We were washing our hands frequently, singing certain songs to time the process. Alcohol wipes and hand sanitisers were constantly being used. We pressed the buttons for street lights or lifts (elevators) with our elbows. On our public transport the railings were constantly sanitised and there were stickers indicating which seats we could sit on to ensure the required 'social distancing'. Mail was left for a couple of days before opening.

Piano teachers thoroughly disinfected the piano keyboard between pupils. Very soon, however, Zoom was being used for all teaching, meetings and consultations. I attended lots of free online information sessions for piano teachers on teaching using Zoom and was most grateful.

I was also extremely pleased that online live exercise classes for seniors were started. I made a point of doing the thirty-minute program each weekday. Medical appointments were either postponed or took place over the telephone. The expiry dates for driving licenses/tests and such were extended, as we could not attend in person.

Basia and my memoir

When the pandemic started, I was just finishing the final draft of my memoir. My friend, Basia, was travelling alone by car through a very remote part of the country in South Australia when all such travel was banned. She wasn't even permitted to drive straight back to her home. Stuck in the middle of nowhere, she luckily found a small caravan park and was able to persuade the owners to allow her to put up a tent and use the amenities. It was some months before she was permitted to drive home. But while 'stuck' and with only her phone for connection, I decided to send her chapters of my book, one at a time. Basia would get into bed in her tent each night and read about my life. When she reached the end of a chapter she would text me and I'd send the next one. I enjoyed being able to provide a little entertainment for her in such isolation, and Basia must have enjoyed the experience as she bought two copies once the book was published. A win/win situation in the face of adversity.

Music and the pandemic

At first, the lockdowns and other restrictions brought out the best in us. Three weeks after lockdown began, the previously busy cities were deserted—videos showed that, in Rome, animals roamed the streets and foliage had begun to engulf the famous monuments—but people started singing from balconies and raising the spirits of not only those near to them but of millions around the world as we watched on Facebook and shared the experiences and emotions. Some of those performers were professionals, some amateurs. Music, whether performed or listened to, was very high on the list for people and communities all over the world. Every opportunity to be creative was taken and people shared whatever they could with others.

Through Facebook, I was able to watch from London the wonderful Canadian/British pianist, Angela Hewitt, as she recorded herself (I think on an iPhone) each day playing music by Bach. Yo-Yo Ma, the cellist, spoke and played every day from his home in the USA. Anthony Hopkins introduced us to his cat, his paintings and his piano playing. Brilliant Australian cellist Rachel Scott began giving regular concerts at extremely affordable prices from her home. Her tech-savvy husband ensured the picture and sound were of excellent quality. World-renowned Australian pianist Simon Tedeschi used an iPhone to record his playing for us. Many others rose to the occasion and shared their talents via social media. Linda Gilbert, a NSW violinist who'd studied in Moscow and was permanently living there, had been visiting her mother in Australia when lockdown began and was unable to return to Russia. She, too, used her phone to give online concerts from 'home'.

Very quickly, two Melbourne musicians started up what is now called the Australian Digital Concert Hall, providing performing opportunities and some income for professional musicians and providing quality, uplifting entertainment for us in lockdown—and afterwards. What began in Melbourne in March 2020 is now nationwide. Some 9,000 musicians and arts industry workers have benefited from these live online concerts. (To date, over $3 million in ticket sales has come from some 550 performances.)

Local restrictions

Our federal government gave the individual state premiers the power to make all decisions about business closures, mask wearing and restrictions of people's movements. Victorians had the longest and most severe restrictions, leading to many protests.

Initially, in New South Wales, we were not permitted to leave home unless it was essential. People were required to work from home if it was possible. It was compulsory to check in and check out of any public places we visited, using an app on our phones. We could shop for essentials (but no browsing was permitted and maintaining social distance was a requirement). Travel was limited to a few kilometers. We could exercise for one hour per day outdoors. In general, children had to be home-schooled. Hairdressers, barbers, beauty salons and many other businesses considered not essential, were forced to close. We were not allowed to hug one another—just elbow contact while wearing masks.

Fortunately the internet in most homes allowed connection with others online—though many of my generation do not have the ability to use smart phones, tablets or computers. For many of today's seniors, the internet is a scary thing.

The losses so many were forced to experience during the pandemic led, in many instances, to an appreciation and joy of many activities previously taken for granted—such simple things as sitting in a park, going for a walk when you felt like it, going to the beach or playground, visiting or spending time with other people, being able to have a massage, attend a cinema or live performances, or sing or dance in a public place. There was also a growing awareness and appreciation of nature in its many forms— the sunsets, sunrises, the birdsong, the movement of the leaves in the trees. When air, sea and road travel were greatly reduced, the skies were much clearer and cleaner, and the sunrises and sunsets became spectacular. Some of my Facebook friends posted daily photos of them—which was certainly a joy.

Development and introduction of COVID 'vaccines'

I've used quotation marks because the products promoted as COVID-19 vaccines are completely different from any previous vaccines. They are said to reduce the severity of the illness, thus reducing the need for hospitalisation, but vaccinated people can still pass on or die of this virus which now has many variants and sub-variants and appears to be more infectious than ever.

None of the vaccines had been fully tested before they began to be used, due to pressure for their early availability. Testing was due to be completed by 2023, so here in Australia, the official approval given in 2021 was for provisional use only.

As soon as these products were developed by the major pharmaceutical companies and became available, our media, churches, and other influential bodies supported the government viewpoint that it was essential we follow the guidelines and be vaccinated. The federal body known as AHPRA (Australian Health Practitioner Regulation Agency) informed all its members that they were not permitted to express anti-COVID vaccination views and that they themselves, if not 'double vaccinated' by the end of October 2021, would be deregistered and lose their jobs. (Health professionals required to be registered with AHPRA include dentists, medical practitioners, nurses and midwives, pharmacists, physiotherapists, psychologists, medical radiation practitioners and occupational therapists.) I found it most interesting to learn (from a video interview with health workers) that some 90 percent of those vaccinated only did so in order to keep their jobs and have restrictions removed. They would not have been injected through choice, but felt coerced.

In August 2021 I watched a video interview with eight leading doctors and scientists from the USA. Most of them had vast experience in treating COVID patients and one had been involved in the production of the vaccine. It was good to be able to see and hear, firsthand, their view that the current vaccines were not the solution and would not put an end to the pandemic. They said the coronavirus was not to be feared because there were treatments available and that if patients were treated early and appropriately, they would not die.

These doctors all used and recommended Ivermectin—a medication which has been used to treat parasites in humans since 1987. Over 5.2 million people had been prescribed Ivermectin since its introduction and it is recorded as being 'gentle and safe and well tolerated'. I also read that a Monash University study found that Ivermectin can kill COVID-19 within forty-eight hours. In the USA more than 88,000 prescriptions for Ivermectin were presented to pharmacies in the week ending 13 August, 2021.

So how odd it was to read a Sydney University statement made on 3 September 2021, saying that Ivermectin was 'an unproven and *potentially dangerous* treatment for COVID-19'. Obviously, there was no 'proven' treatment for COVID-19, as it was a completely new disease. But Ivermectin was being used widely in other countries, and many people chose to buy the animal formulations of the product online or over the counter, and self-treated, sometimes overdosing.

At the same time, our TV stations were not only screening paid government advertisements—they were also showing TV personalities urging us to be vaccinated. The message being broadcast was that to be vaccinated was in the interest of the well-being of others and of helping put an end to the global pandemic. As I write this, Australia has the highest percentage of vaccinated people in the world, and COVID cases are still rapidly spreading around the country.

Local restrictions/my situation

Since 1963 I've chosen to follow a natural health regime, eating whole fresh unrefined foods in general, and mostly abstaining from alcohol, tea and coffee. I've never tried any illegal drug. I've chosen not to have a microwave oven. I don't take painkillers or other medications. I gave birth to three children naturally (with only a naturopathic nurse in attendance). I don't have injections when my teeth are filled. I've not had cervical smears or mammograms or annual flu injections. I would not say yes to any medication unless it was essential or compulsory. And so it was my choice not to have any COVID-19 injections.

My decision led to increased restrictions and several disappointments. I was not allowed to go to a hairdresser or other shops once they reopened in December 2021. This year I was stopped from getting on a community bus for my first social outing since the start of the COVID pandemic as it was regarded as putting others in danger. My family felt they couldn't visit, as they would be putting me in danger.

However, I've been one of the lucky ones. Living alone and independently, I have complete choice of my activities in a comfortable apartment in a retirement village. I'm receiving an aged pension, which covers my government-subsidised rent, food, clothing etc. I know how to use devices to order my food and other items online. Most importantly, I'm happy with my own company. When I'm not writing I spend my days reading and communicating with friends (and strangers) online or via phone/texts. I play the piano daily and practice pieces I might be permitted to play, one day, in the Common Room here, to entertain the other residents. I love playing word games and play 'Upwords', a Scrabble-like game, on my iPad. I'm lucky to have outdoor balconies where I can sit in the fresh air and sunshine.

COVID restrictions lifted or relaxed

Some restrictions were lifted in NSW in December 2021, when 95 percent of the population had received at least one vaccination. Vaccinated people were permitted to visit cinemas, beauty salons, cafes or restaurants and attend certain events—provided they wore face masks and maintained social distance.

But by the beginning of 2022, millions of people worldwide (tradespeople and professionals alike) were taking physical action as they protested about the enforced vaccinations and restrictions. Here in Australia, thousands of medical professionals and teachers, along with firefighters and lifesavers (volunteers at beaches) were among those who've *not* been permitted to continue to work due to not being vaccinated. I have friends who lost their jobs; friends who became 'outcasts' in the eyes of their families and friends; friends who were banned from Facebook.

On 8 June, 2022, the new NSW Premier said, 'I've made it very clear that we are ending vaccine mandates'. He added that he'd asked top bureaucrats to remove mandates from the workforce. However, it is still the case that I cannot sing with a local choir unless I have a certificate to show I'm 'fully vaccinated'. I think it's now up to three additional boosters. There is still much discrimination, and many people are suffering as a result.

Back on 18 November, 2021, Australia's then prime minister, Scott Morrison, said that the government's position was that vaccines should only be mandatory in very specific circumstances. He stated: 'Vaccines are only mandatory in cases where you've got health workers that are working alongside vulnerable people. That's what our medical advice has always been.' Yet thousands of school teachers were not allowed to work unless they were vaccinated. And unvaccinated airline pilots, truck drivers, builders, and many others who were not working alongside vulnerable people were all suspended or lost their jobs. Novak Djokovic was not permitted to play at the Australian Open as it was believed he was a danger—his decision not to be vaccinated could lead to others doing the same.

Recent developments

In Australia, in September 2022, it was officially stated that the latest strain of COVID (Omicron BA.5) posed a significant new threat, and we were instructed again to work from home and wear masks indoors. And just a few days later, it was announced that the BA.2.75 variant had hit Australia. Then, at the beginning of November, the new variants BQ1 and XBB were tipped to become of major concern with the numbers of cases expected to increase. In the midst of all this, the World Health Organisation declared the Monkeypox virus a global emergency in order that vaccines can swiftly be made available.

Despite Australia's high rate of vaccination, the Immunisation Research Centre recently announced that well over 60 percent of adults and children have been infected with COVID-19.

Conspiracy theories

Since the beginning of the COVID pandemic, many people have been circulating and discussing the theory that the World Health Organisation, the United Nations, the World Bank, some of the world's wealthiest people and many others in positions of power are planning a 'New World Order'. There are claims that the coronavirus was deliberately produced and the vaccines were designed to control and alter humanity. There are a number of different conspiracy theories. One such theory, believed by many people, is that we are experiencing the biblical Apocalypse (the final book of the New Testament). Earlier this year I saw a clever cartoon where a library had a sign indicating that books on *the Apocalypse* were now to be found under *Current Affairs.*

The literal meaning of the word Apocalypse is 'revelation of great knowledge'. Many Christians believe it refers to the complete destruction of the world, preceding the establishment of a new world and heaven—an 'end time' scenario.

I find it interesting that the Apocalypse is commonly considered to be an event or chain of events *detrimental* to humanity and the planet. The world prior to the pandemic was so far from perfect! The air and seas were polluted. The earth was being ripped apart by mining, and trees were being felled for unsustainable farming. The environment was being damaged severely for financial reasons.

Those in power and positions of leadership were not basing their decisions on the interests of the people—their motivation was the desire to keep control, to make more money, to help their friends. The political systems had made it well-nigh impossible for politicians to act with compassion and care. In my view, *major change* is essential and desirable.

2. POLITICS

Politics in Australia

A few years ago I was in a small writing class where we were given a topic to write about each month. On one occasion the subject was politics, and without exception, each one of us expressed similar sentiments. Here is some of what I wrote at the time. (July 2017)

'I don't regularly watch or listen to news programs or read newspapers. However, I take very seriously any opportunities to vote or give my input. I watch the TV debates before elections and 'look up' the various candidates.

At a local level, I take an interest in council decisions, though I no longer choose to be involved in local or federal 'consultations', having experienced several where outcomes had been decided in advance and much money was wasted on giving the impression that the public's views were being considered.

In my opinion, Australia's political system is not a good one. With opposing parties, much energy, manpower, time and money are spent trying to pull down the other main party. It would seem that gaining power or staying in power far outweighs any other considerations. At elections, I have problems when my preferred local candidate belongs to a party I know can't win. Election promises are traditionally broken and can't be believed. Recently, it's been the party leader, and whether I want to see him or her in or out, that has determined my vote or preferences. I'd really like to see our politicians working together to provide the best services possible.

On many subjects my views are far removed from those of most, if not all, of our politicians. I believe that no party or politician should ever be permitted to accept donations or any other favours from another person, business or country. I do not accept the claim that this money is necessary for informing and communicating with the public. Free publicity is readily available to the government through radio, TV and the internet, and we no longer need expensive TV advertisements or posted mailouts to every constituent, nor do individual members need to be using taxpayer money for professionally made videos of themselves. Ministers should 'minister'. And all politicians' expenses should be just that—not scales of allowances or perks for life.

More importantly, I'm a pacifist. I don't believe that warfare is the way to solve any problem. Physical violence can actually create greater problems. I believe in the Golden Rule of treating others as we'd like to be treated— a far cry from how our politicians treat refugees, so-called 'illegal' immigrants, criminals, and possible or potential terrorists. It follows that I'm also not in favour of any sanctions imposed on other countries or regimes, or of 'condemning' others for their supposed wrongdoings.

I'd love to see a return to non-privatisation—where the government uses taxpayers' money to provide all the important services such as transport, banking, communication by post and telephone, electricity, and gas. In my view, the sale of government assets to companies intending to make money for their shareholders is a counterproductive and unacceptable practice.

I remember many years ago reading a report that showed that the government would actually save money if all rail transport was free of charge. The overall cost of printing, inspecting and collecting tickets was then greater than the income derived. I sometimes wonder how that would work out today if we got rid of Opal, electronic barriers and inspectors! Loss of jobs, of course, but maybe those people could answer phones—and I don't mean in call centres; it would be wonderful if they could answer them in government departments.

Shortage of jobs is of course, one of today's major problems, yet manpower is needed in so many places. Our government puts money into forms of job creation that don't work in the long run, but are very costly. And it claims that more coal mines will mean more jobs. For me, the ends never justify the means. Before slavery was abolished, job loss was given as a reason for voting against the proposed legislation and keeping the status quo.

'Economic growth' is another subject that disturbs me. Some forty years ago I read some books on the subject, which showed clearly how undesirable it is to seek economic growth. Politicians are still talking about economic growth. There seems to be a connotation of increased prosperity.

Fortunately, in Australia we have a variety of non-government groups and voluntary services that minister to those in need. They seem to bring out the best in people, and to build community. We need more of that and an end to the fear and distrust of each other that our politicians often seem to encourage.

I look forward to future developments in technology enabling us to have much simpler forms of government, with fewer politicians truly ministering and serving the public and making decisions that are in the best interests of the people they serve.'

Since I wrote those words, there have been major changes to Australia's political scene. At the May 2022 federal elections, voters made it quite clear that the Liberal, Morrison-led government was not what they wanted. The change this time was that a number of new, strong independent candidates worked together with good financial backing and publicity. Known as Teal Independents, their policies were part Green (environmentalists) and part blue (Liberal Party). People voted for them and for the Greens. Labour's Anthony Albanese, our new Prime Minister, acknowledged that they'd heard the message from voters—Australians wanted more action on climate change and renewable energy, and an end to the lies, pork-barreling, etc.

A new era has begun for us. Relationships with other countries have been 'repaired'. Some major 'humanitarian' problems have been resolved. Our new government got off to an impressive start—apparently basing decisions on the wellbeing of the country and its people. While I'm not in agreement with some of the policies, I'm delighted with this change for the better, though it's staggering to learn that Australia's debt is due to exceed $1 trillion next year. (I've read that the risk of a global recession is growing with fifty-four nations urgently requiring debt relief to stop poverty levels from rising.)

Global Politics

Since the pandemic began, there have been major changes in leadership in many countries, some sudden and unexpected.

The second Elizabethan Age came to an end with the death of Queen Elizabeth II on 8 September, 2022. Queen Elizabeth had devotedly served and reigned for over seventy years. The two thousand guests at her funeral in Westminster Abbey included kings, queens, presidents, prime ministers, celebrities and friends from across the globe. Her son Charles is now king of the United Kingdom and the Commonwealth. The coronation of King Charles III and Camilla, Queen Consort, is to take place on 8 May, 2023.

In the USA elections in 2020, Biden defeated Trump, though Trump refused to concede the election, alleging widespread voter fraud, and mounting more than sixty unsuccessful legal challenges in several states.

In Myanmar, the military seized power in 2021, and was reported to have killed over 2,000 protesters and arrested some 15,000. The Nobel prize winner, Aung San Suu Kyi, who won the 2020 election, was placed under house arrest and sentenced to eleven years in jail. In mid-August, a number of Myanmar's pro-democracy campaigners were executed, and six years were added to the eleven-year jail sentence of Aung San Suu Kyi.

The relationship between China and Taiwan became fraught as the USA strengthened ties with Taiwan.

There was violence and death during the elections in Papua New Guinea.

The flight and resignation of the president of Sri Lanka brought that country to its knees.

In July, after months of political turmoil, the president of Italy resigned.

Kahn was ousted as Pakistan's leader. He said his refusal to be 'a puppet by the West' caused him to be singled out and led to his loss of support. Subsequently, there was an attempt on his life.

In the UK, prime minister Boris Johnson was forced to stand down. Liz Truss was elected to replace him, and had her official meeting with Queen Elizabeth II, two days before the long-serving and much loved monarch's death. Just six weeks later, Truss's economic plan was 'shredded' and she was forced to resign. On 25 October, 2022, Rishi Sunak became the first British Asian prime minister.

In Afghanistan, Syria and Israel, the ongoing warfare and fighting has intensified this year. Twelve months after the Taliban took control of Afghanistan, the economy was in a state of collapse. Almost all Afghans are living below the poverty line, human rights abuses are running rampant and thousands are trying to get to Australia.

The most world-changing event began on 24 February this year, when Russia invaded Ukraine. Putin claimed they were merely seeking to free Russians living in there, announcing it as a special military operation for the demilitarisation and 'denazification' of Ukraine. But as civilians were wounded and killed, there was a strong and immediate reaction throughout the world, with many countries applying sanctions and ceasing to trade with Russia. Ukraine's President Zelenskyy reached out for financial and military help and gained support from many countries. Africa, Asia, and the Middle East were badly affected when Ukraine's ports were blocked by Russia, resulting in the cessation of exports of wheat and other products.

Casualties on both sides have been horrendous. In July, it was estimated that 15,000 Russians had been killed and another 45,000 wounded. The figures for Ukraine adults were not known, but are much lower; at least 423 Ukrainian children have been killed, 811 wounded and 239 have been reported missing. Over 7.6 million refugees (mostly women and children) have so far escaped the Ukraine war—a quarter of the country's population leaving their homes in the first month. To date (19 October, 2022), there have been at least 623 attacks on vital health services, and 30 percent of Ukraine's power stations have been destroyed. Last month, Ukraine's nuclear power plant lost its remaining link to the main power line. The US, alone, has so far provided nearly $18 billion in military aid as the fighting continues.

I must admit that I'm amazed at this whole situation. I know a massive amount of money is made from the sale of weapons and from war, generally. I know warfare has been the traditional way for countries to behave when there are disagreements. But I really expected today's world leaders (or their advisors) to be aware that violence begets violence—it doesn't create peace. And that condemnation, sanctions and punishments are counterproductive—they inflame the fire and invariably hurt the one applying them. The United Nations, with its mission statement *Peace, dignity and equality on a healthy planet*, seems unable to help. Former Trump advisor Fiona Hill said recently 'Putin must be contained, but that won't happen unless and until international institutions established in the wake of World War II evolve so they *can* contain him.' It looks as if it might take World War III to bring that about.

3. NATURAL DISASTERS

Along with these 'man-made' disasters, we have also experienced severe and frequent 'natural disasters' this year—devastating fires, floods, tsunamis, earthquakes and landslides. My heart goes out to the millions of people who've been impacted by these events.

In Pakistan, over 33 million people were displaced by floodwaters and landslides between June and late August. With one-third of the country under water, a state of national emergency was declared. At least 1,400 people lost their lives in the floods as the torrential rains swept away thousands of homes, roads, railways, livestock and crops.

Bangladesh and India have experienced the worst floods in decades. In Bangladesh about four million people were cut off and needed help.

Five million people in India were affected by the Brahmaputra River breaking its banks, submerging villages, destroying crops and wrecking homes.

More than 500,000 people in China were evacuated due to flooding.

In June, a major earthquake in Afghanistan killed at least 1,000 people. More than 1,500 people were injured, and there was extensive damage to homes and buildings.

A volcano in Tonga shattered the country's only fibre optic cable, resulting in no phone or internet services being available for a whole month.

Australia, too, has had record flooding, with some people having been evacuated from their homes four times this year. Sydney is set to surpass its all-time rainfall record. I read today of nurses having to use boats to reach the hospital in the Central West town of Forbes (NSW).

I believe people will look back one day and realise that the planet itself was clearly indicating the need for its custodians to make changes in their behaviour. Just as we might have severe temperature fluctuations (hot one minute, cold the next) or other obvious physical signs that all is not well and we need to rest, take care of our body, and make changes to our behaviour, so too is our beautiful planet indicating her great distress. There's a desperate need for care and respect for planet Earth, cessation of unnecessary mining, destruction of trees and forests, and pollution of seas, rivers, oceans, air, and ground.

The physical environment is the one subject the British monarchy has spoken about publicly. Members of the Royal Family do not express opinions on problems or world affairs, but it was reported that the late queen did encourage some world leaders to take part in the Glasgow Climate Summit in October 2021. It is heartening to know that King Charles and his sons are passionate about the broad range of environmental changes currently taking place.

CHAPTER 12

An Ending

I had no idea when I began writing this book of how it would change *me*.

As I've focussed my attention on my own experiences and responses, I've been amazed at just how incredible and powerful we are. Everything we experience—whether it be what we see, hear, smell, taste or feel—is affected by us. We influence what is seemingly outside of us, and the main way we do this is through our attitude to it, our intention, our expectation, our beliefs. Those things determine the vibes we give out and influence everything we perceive.

We have a great deal of choice as to what we experience. And we have unlimited options as to how we respond to each of our experiences. We can make a big deal of it or be lighthearted and grateful—and everything in between. We can analyse and pay attention to difficulties and problems past, present and future, or, when triggered, just stop, relax, quieten the mind and focus on what we're actually feeling until the emotion has run its course.

I've constantly had my emotions triggered this year, and I have been taking my own advice to stop and feel, without thinking about it, until inner peace is restored. I used to say in my head 'I'm feeling this frustration' (or whatever) until the feeling passed. I couldn't always identify the emotion but could always feel it in my body—the gut or lower belly as a rule. Since writing that, however, I've come across a method that works even better for me.

After seeing a Facebook comment about releasing emotions using *The Sedona Method,* I looked it up and bought Hale Dwoskin's book on the subject. I've only read two chapters so far, and stopped (as directed) to practice and to make notes of issues that I'd like to feel better about—would like to change or improve in my life.

It's been magical for me. Now when I feel any uncomfortable emotion, I merely ask myself, *Can I welcome this feeling? Can I allow it?* By then, it's usually dissipated and I'm smiling. There are three more questions, but I've only asked them twice *(Could I let it go? Would I let it go? When?)* I find this more fun than my previous more serious approach, and I look forward to reading the rest of Dwoskin's book.

* * *

When I was a child, back in the 1930s and 1940s, we had no fear of 'strangers'—of people we didn't know. Children played away from home and walked to and from school with freedom. Most homes were not locked. We always had the key in the front door when someone was home. But time has taken its toll.

Today there are many people who are disturbed and perverted as a result of their own upbringing and experiences. There is much pain—and it is being expressed by violent behaviour of various kinds.

Many of us now regard others with suspicion. The phone will not be answered unless it's from a known caller. Tiny tots are taught not to talk to strangers. Children are told about others touching them, and how to respond. It seems that many of them are taken directly to school and collected afterwards purely because of fear of what others might do.

The lack of trust in our fellow man is easily spread. It's a learned behaviour. These same people who are suspicious of others will automatically 'lend a hand' in times of emergency and obvious need. They will happily help friends and neighbours in the event of illness or misfortune. They will generously contribute money— even if they have little—to support those who've lost homes and possessions in bushfires or floods or other natural disasters. At heart, people today are loving, kind and generous, and will put the well-being of others before their own. But fear has crept in, and hearts have hardened as a protective measure.

It is some 2,000 years since Jesus left a legacy to mankind to love God, to love one another, to love ourselves, to let go of fear, to have faith that our needs will be met, to forgive those who have wronged us, to treat others as we'd like to be treated, not to judge others… The Old Testament dwelt on fear. The New Testament was based on the life and teachings of Jesus, who focused on love and non-judgement.

If humans are to evolve into a state of loving and caring for one another and the environment, we have a lot of change to undergo. But, of course, all of this can be seen as a challenge—and an opportunity for healing—which is how I regard it.

***

While I've long held the opinion that everything and everyone is as they need to be—that everyone is doing the best they can, that everything that happens to us can be used for benefit, and that it helps to give thanks and be grateful for everything—I'd not had the complete and comfortable acceptance of every event and every person. I'd prayed for all leaders, but I was also judgemental of some of them. I'd 'accepted' my recent major physical limitations, but I was trying to change them.

Early this morning, I scrolled through some Facebook posts and was reminded of our family's attitude to Father Christmas. When my sister and I were tiny, we were told that Father Christmas was pretend, as was the story of the reindeer, elves, coming down the chimney, etc. We were used to games of pretend and were happy to learn that this was one that even adults played. Mummys and Daddys pretended to be Santa and put their children's presents in their Christmas stockings (or pillowslips). We tried to stay awake to see our parents doing it, but they always waited until we were asleep. My sister and I, in turn, used to be Santa to our parents and as soon as we woke on Christmas Day we crept into their room and left presents at the foot of their bed before enjoying the fruitcake, carrots and drink they'd placed on the dressing table for Santa and his helpers. We had been told, though, that not every child knew it was pretend, so we were not to spoil it for any of our friends.

So, why was I reminded of this by seeing normal Facebook posts? Well, it all seemed 'unreal'. I suddenly *felt* that life in the physical world is like a stage play. I was both observing it and playing a role in it—and learning every day how to be more confident and comfortable in my role.

For much of my life I've regarded living as a burden. I'd have preferred not to be here. Most of the time I have looked forward to my current experiences being over, so that I could have better ones. After I recently decided to work full-time Mondays to Fridays on the final draft of this book, I had many thoughts of the freedoms I believed the weekend would bring. I found myself looking forward to the lack of set hours, the lack of 'work', the opportunity to do whatever I wished. It was funny. The first weekend I felt 'lost', as if adrift at sea.

I soon realised that I was blessed and privileged to have *all* the opportunities that living on Earth offers. 'The good and the bad and the ugly' are all gifts for us to enjoy. Just as it is possible to enjoy a film that might contain conflict, destruction or sadness—and cry along with it or have our hearts uplifted by it—so we can accept and be grateful for every single thing that we experience here on Earth.

We have little control over what thoughts pop into our head or what feelings arise as we experience life in this physical world. But we do have choice in regard to whether we pursue the thought or discard it, whether we feel the feeling, bottle it up or express it through behaviour that could harm others.

We have endless choices about what we look at, what we listen to, what we eat and drink, what we touch and feel and what we smell, and, most importantly, what we visualise and what we put into words. We can choose joy, whenever the opportunity arises. We can learn new skills and change old habits to increase our joy in life. We can look with fresh eyes at ourselves, at one another, and at the amazing and wonderful world around us.